Cases for Middle School Educators

Theresa Gayle Siskind

The Scarecrow Press, Inc.
Technomic Books
Lanham, Maryland, and London
2000

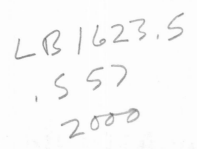
SCARECROW PRESS, INC.
Technomic Books

Published in the United States of America
by Scarecrow Press, Inc.
4720 Boston Way
Lanham, Maryland 20706
http://www.scarecrowpress.com

4 Pleydell Gardens, Folkestone
Kent CT20 2DN, England

British Library Cataloguing in Publication Information Available

Library of Congress Cataloging-in-Publication Data

Siskind, Theresa Gayle, 1951–
    Cases for middle school educators / Theresa Gayle Siskind.
        p. cm.
    Includes index.
    ISBN 0-8108-3762-5 (pbk. : alk. paper)
    1. Middle schools—United States—Case studies. 2. Middle school teachers—United
States—Case studies. I. Title.

LB1623.5 .S57 2000
373.236'0973—dc21   99-086734

This book is dedicated to my son, Bryan, whose middle school experiences inspired my interest.

CONTENTS

FOREWORD

This book is not *my* book. It belongs to the educators who authored it, whose stories it retells. These consummate professionals share their experiences in an endeavor to enhance the profession. Their cases provide a basis for reflection and growth.

Many of these cases grew out of the Middle School Project, an experimental program for training middle school teachers, which linked an extraordinarily talented group of practicing teachers with an extraordinarily talented group of Masters in Teaching (MAT) students. I was extraordinarily lucky to have been a part of the process. The reflection and growth that the cases stimulated as part of the project was not limited to the teachers and students involved. They stimulated my thoughts as they continue to do every time I read them.

These cases are true stories. Although a few details may have been altered to protect the identities of the people involved, they are essentially the recollection and recitation of the educators who lived them. I value and cherish their memories and their willingness to share the stories so that we may all grow and develop as professionals and people.

The cases in this book are appropriate for discussion by in-service professionals as well as preservice professionals, by administrators as well as teachers. Although the cases all emphasize middle-level decision making and the middle-level professional and student, their messages are applicable to other levels as well.

ACKNOWLEDGMENTS

This project was supported in part by grants from the Citadel Development Foundation and the South Carolina Center for Excellence in Accelerated Learning.

Introduction

My personal philosophy has been shaped by my own experience as a teacher at the "middle school" level, as the parent of a child who endured three years in a "middle school," and as the director of the Middle School Project. The Middle School Project was my redemption. It taught me that there are good and true middle schools where children learn and develop and that, unlike my own teacher preparation program, teacher training programs can prepare middle school teachers well. My philosophy is guided by the Turning Points report. In properly structured middle schools with adequate administrative support in order that transescents and young adolescents can experience self-exploration and self-definition and have meaningful school participation with positive social interactions, students can achieve and grow in all domains. I have witnessed how effective teaming and interdisciplinary units and other middle school "outgrowths" can be. Of course, not every interaction and innovation is successful. Awareness can smooth the route to becoming a middle school teacher; and awareness may be achieved through reading, reflection, and discussion.

Cases, especially real cases, can paint a picture of school life. Stories about people and their dilemmas are often more interesting than theory or methods texts. They bring life to the theory and checklists that students are given. Cases should not be used too early in an instructional sequence, but once students have developed the knowledge base, case analysis allows them to practice problem solving, to apply their previous knowledge, to mesh theory and practice, to simulate situations, to consult with others and work on collaborative solutions, to think and rethink, and to be active, constructive learners.

Case discussions can form the basis for in-service training or informal study groups by practicing teachers and administrators. They can be used in team-building exercises. They invigorate. They stimulate thought and they force professionals to think about their practice. Practicing educators are no less enthusiastic about cases than preservice educators.

The remainder of this introductory chapter will briefly detail the history of adolescence, trace the history of the middle school and describe the current conception, reiterate current concepts of adolescence, and define case-based instruction. A final section ties the cases to the *Standards for School Leaders*. Each of the following nineteen chapters will present a case followed by discussion questions.

A BRIEF HISTORY OF ADOLESCENCE

The word "adolescence" derives from the Latin "adolescere"—to grow up. Adolescence is generally recognized as a period of increasing independence from puberty onward. It has been characterized as the "liminal stage between childhood and adulthood" (Hanawalt 1992, p. 343). Springhall (1986) notes:

> It is curious that while "childlike" usually connotes as much praise as "adult," the adjectival use of "adolescent" is strictly pejorative. Thus whereas to be "childlike" means to be full of wonder and freshness and "adult" means to be mature and responsible, to be "adolescent" generally means to be juvenile, vulgar, self-important and often just plain silly in behaviour. (p. 1)

Although the first uses of the word can be found in medieval texts, common usage is attributed to the fin de siècle period and beyond. The study of adolescence was pioneered by the work of G. Stanley Hall, an American "alienist" who was strongly influenced by Darwinian recapitulation theories, according to Demos and Demos (1969).

The development of adolescence was an outgrowth of the Industrial Revolution and increasing urbanization (Demos and Demos 1969; Gillis 1974; Hanawalt 1992; Springhall 1986). Industrialization contributed to adolescence by fostering economic independence from the family unit. Its accompanying urbanization brought families in close contact with one another, enabling the growth of peer groups. The peer group usurped the socialization function, formerly the province of parents and adult society.

According to Aries (1962, p. 29), in preindustrial Europe "people had no idea of what we call adolescence." Some contend that this life stage was called "youth." Youth "was a very long transition period, lasting from the point that the very young child first became somewhat independent of its family, usually about seven or eight, to the point of complete independence at marriage, ordinarily in the mid- or late twenties" (Gillis 1974, p. 2). In addition to its extraordinary length by current standards, youth was not demarcated by age transitions. In fact, "many people . . . did not know their own exact age" (Kett 1977, p. 13). Prior to the nineteenth century, schooling was not mandatory so school age did not mark a particular transition. There were no shifts in clothing that would signify age transitions. Many children left home to work at an early age (seven or eight), so not living with one's family did not indicate a particular maturational stage. In fact, actual physical growth and the onset of puberty occurred several years later than the modern-day onset due to nutritional deficiencies (Gillis 1974).

Toward the latter part of the Victorian period, there was a tendency to control the size of the middle-class family. This became an important contributor to the development of interest in childhood and adolescence. Earlier families had been large. As infant mortality dropped, an increasing number of "redundant" children abounded and family limitation became important (Gillis 1974, p. 21). With fewer children came a greater interest in the children that one did have. The importance of secondary school as a time of dependent adolescence is emphasized by both Gillis (1974) and Neubauer (1991), much as college matriculation has extended adolescence in present-day society.

Common use, or disuse, of the word "adolescence" has sparked historical debate (Hanawalt 1992). Some historians claim that without linguistic recognition (prior to the late nineteenth century), the construct of adolescence did not exist. Others argue that the existence of the construct was not bound by the existence of the word. These opposing views are mediated somewhat by the call for a distinction between biological and cultural constructions of adolescence.

A BRIEF HISTORY OF THE MIDDLE SCHOOL

The middle school evolved as the differentiation of school levels evolved. During the early years of American education in the agrarian, relatively underpopulated rural areas, differentiation of school levels was unnecessary. The concept of the one-room schoolhouse embodies this era.

With the advent of industrialization, urbanization, and increasingly dense settlement, public schooling took on the mission of providing a basic education for its populace. Most students terminated school at a time coincidental to the advent of adolescence. A few students continued their education in specialized private preparatory schools or colleges. This system eventually developed into two distinct levels of schooling: elementary or grammar and high school. The predominant, though not exclusive, configuration was eight years of grammar school and four years of high school.

Around the beginning of the twentieth century, several movements converged to promote the establishment of junior high schools. Legislation required students to remain in school until the age of fourteen. The high school, which was originally conceived as a college preparatory unit, did not provide the curriculum needed by most students going into the world of work. Elementary schooling began to be conceived of as too long and not related to the needs of older pupils.

The junior high school proliferated with the post–World War I birthrate, immigration, and urbanization. In the 1960s, the middle school movement was born from questions about whether the junior high school was meeting student needs. These needs encompassed physical, cognitive, and socioemotional development.

In the twenty-year period from 1967–68 to 1987–88 the total number of middle schools increased 500 percent (Alexander and McEwin 1989); however, much of this growth was not directly related to student needs. Desegregation and changing demographic patterns played a large role in the 1960s and 1970s. In the 1980s, research on schooling also provided an impetus. Reports like *A Nation at Risk* (National Commission on Excellence in Education 1983) challenged the fundamental quality of American education and forced educators at all levels to reconceptualize their missions and methods.

During this period of time research into middle school practices and general characteristics of the transescent began to have an impact as well. One of the most influential reports, *Turning Points: Preparing American Youth for the 21st Century,* reemphasized the needs of adolescents in the middle school. Among the suggestions were the following: small communities for learning; attention to physical, social, and emotional health of students; attention to the academic program; involvement of parents and the community in education; and specialized training for middle-level educators.

The middle school, unlike the content-centered junior high school, is student centered. Its organizational structure emphasizes cross-disciplinary teams with integrated curricula rather than departmentalization. Recognizing the cognitive, physical, and socioemotional changes in transescents, it emphasizes active exploratory learning activities set within a flexible schedule. Advisory programs are an integral part of the learner-centered focus.

A BRIEF OVERVIEW: MIDDLE-LEVEL LEARNERS

Physical Development

Although certainly characterized by individual differences, adolescence is characterized by growth spurts. Adolescence is a period of rapid and visible body changes. Skeletal and muscular changes are accompanied by sexual reproductive changes. Many students grow taller and heavier and more sexually developed. Growing pains can be a reality. This rapid change may be scary and confusing for students who are developing as well as those who are watching their classmates develop while they appear to lag behind.

Socioemotional Development

Rapid physical growth is naturally accompanied by curiosity and some trepidation. A preoccupation with the developing self often develops. In addition, adolescence is characterized by a shift in social dependence from family to peers. Peers set the standards for dress, thinking, and social action. Same sex friendships replace familial ties; later, cross-sex relationships begin to supersede same-sex friendships.

Cognitive Development

The theoretical grounding for adolescent cognitive development has centered around Piagetian theories. Chronologically, adolescents straddle the concrete operational phase and the formal operational phase. In the concrete operational stage, students can comprehend and apply principles but only when they are attached to concrete examples. Abstraction is not achieved until the formal operational period. Like all development, however, cognitive development is not smooth, continuous, or universal. Individual differences and spurty growth likely characterize cognitive development as well as physical and socioemotional development.

More recent cognitive theories emphasize the social nature of cognition. The value of the social context of learning and the interrelationship of physical, cognitive, and socioemotional changes are recognized in social cognition. Adolescent egocentrism is based on social context, as is perspective taking. Adolescent egocentrism manifests itself in comments by adolescents like, "What are you looking at?" Perspective-taking refers to the developmental process by which adolescents become aware of other points of view. Cognitive theories have great implications for how instruction is best designed for adolescents. Concrete examples accompanied by practice with abstract reasoning, collaborative exercises, and personalized tasks are all implicated. A valuable exercise would include brainstorming other techniques.

CASE-BASED INSTRUCTION

Teacher education is often viewed as "unbearably generic, offering vague general principles and maxims that purport to apply broadly to a vast range of situations" (Shulman 1996, p. 198). Cases, on the other hand, are said to provide a meaningful context for reflective practice (Shulman 1996), which bridges theory and practice, the role of a student preparing to teach with the role of the teacher (Colbert, Trimble, and Desberg, 1996). Casebooks, like this one, reiterate the premise that reading, discussing, and writing cases help teachers and prospective teachers develop, clarify, and solidify their teaching philosophies (Harrington and Garrison 1992; Shulman 1991, 1992).

In a recent follow-up evaluation of the Middle School Project, teachers, who had been students during the project, were asked how the case discussions affected their development as teachers. A sampling of responses follows:

> I already had an understanding of how to address certain situations that you wouldn't normally have any training for. . . . I know first year teachers, who [had] those problems came up and they didn't know how to react. . . . So I had, at least, a basis to understand problems that might occur with middle school students, or even any other high school class, and how to deal with it. Something they don't teach you out of a book. (BK, pp. 4–5)
>
> I think it helped broaden your base going into the classroom. You kind of understand the process. (DR, p. 4)
>
> I've seen some of those kinds of cases we talked about. Some of those were extreme, but I've seen some like it actually happen here with students. (MB, p. 3)
>
> And so whenever I was faced with some similar cases in my teaching, at least I had something to draw on. (ST, p. 2)

The use of these cases will be most effective if students/participants read them ahead of the appointed discussion time and spend some time in individual reflection. Prior to a large-group discussion, paired or small group discussion is recommended. Dramatizing the cases is also effective. The last case, "The Team," is especially amenable to "acting out."

The discussion questions are starters for reflection and discussion. Do not be limited to these seedlings of questions. Similarly, do not be limited to reading and discussing the cases. Writing case analyses and writing cases are important synthesizing experiences. In the words of one of the "authors":

> Oh, goodness, it really made me take an objective look at what happened. It made me look at my biases toward the situation and . . . say, "Is that what happened?" (MC, p. 2)

As in real life, cases have multiple layers and multiple solutions. To constrict and define cases too narrowly restricts their value. In recognition of their multifaceted nature, these cases have not been categorized by topic. In every good reflective exercise, the value of all (reasonable) observations and points of view must be recognized.

FOR SCHOOL LEADERS

Like these cases, the role of school administrator is not linear and one-dimensional. In 1996, *Standards for School Leaders*, a document prepared by the Interstate School Leaders License Consortium (ISLLC) was adopted. It outlines a set of common standards and defines leadership:

> Effective school leaders are strong educators, anchoring their work on central issues of learning and teaching and school improvement. They are moral agents and social advocates for the children and the communities they serve. Finally, they make strong connections with other people, valuing and caring for others as individuals and as members of the educational community. (p. 2)

The *Standards*, which are reprinted in the appendix, reflect commitments to:

- A willingness to continuously examine one's own assumptions, beliefs, and practices (Standard 1);
- Continuous school improvement (Standard 1);
- Professional development as an integral part of school improvement (Standard 2);
- Human resources management and development (Standard 3);

- Bringing ethical principles to the decision-making process (Standard 5);
- Recognizing a variety of ideas, values, and cultures (Standard 6);
- Importance of a continuing dialogue with other decision makers affecting education (Standard 6)

Use of the cases in this book would facilitate the accomplishment of these and other standards. The cases can be used in formal and informal leadership training programs. School leaders can utilize these cases in faculty development, team building, and communication development exercises. Recognizing the value of these cases for school leaders, a section at the end of each case focuses specifically on the school leader.

CHAPTER ONE

Catherine Conner

It was Catherine Conner's first year at Pine Creek Middle School. The year looked to be promising. For the first time the school was going to be staffed with an administrator and a guidance counselor for each grade. The faculty was energetic. There were many young teachers on staff with fresh ideas and the veteran teachers were ready to guide them along. Catherine was excited about coming to a school with a good reputation, and Pine Creek Middle was on an uphill climb. The school had certainly seen harder times.

Just five years prior to Catherine's arrival, the school was shrouded with negative publicity when an eighth-grade girl was murdered as she took a shortcut through the woods on her way to the suburban school one morning. Another student was suspected of the crime, but no one had ever been charged. The conservative, middle-class community was in an uproar as a flood of police officers and reporters inundated the school. The school was eventually excused of any responsibility, but Catherine knew how hard it had been for them to overcome the blight of the case. The future looked good for Pine Creek Middle.

On the first day of school, the new faculty members were introduced to one another and to the rest of the staff. Catherine was surprised to discover that the new administrator, Ms. Goodwine, had been placed in the seventh grade, the grade in which Catherine would be teaching. She had always heard that seventh grade was an especially turbulent level, and it seemed logical to her that a more experienced administrator would be needed to handle that difficult grade. After all, the seventh grade was the largest grade in the school, and the new administrator had no previous school experience except her administrative internship. Catherine was concerned about the administrative support, but she did not feel it was her place to ask questions. She was a new teacher in a new place and did not yet know in whom she could confide.

The year began smoothly. Catherine was learning the ropes of the middle school and working on a team, something she had not been exposed to during her year of teaching high school. Catherine had made it a practice to try to get to know her students individually as early in the year as possible. She felt that knowing about them as individuals would help her understand how to deal with each student more appropriately. She had the opportunity to learn about one girl even before school began.

Teaming

Middle school teams are usually comprised of an identified group of students and their subject matter teachers. Although students change classes, the number of class changes and the number of teachers and other students to which they are exposed is limited. The concept is designed to promote cohesiveness and support—the student is not just another face in the crowd; he or she is a member of the group recognized and known by the other members of the group.

Oftentimes the academic teachers of the team have a common planning period (in addition to an individual planning period) that they can utilize to plan and coordinate instruction, classroom management, and other issues. Student needs and problems may be jointly addressed.

She met Jenny at registration. Jenny was a sweet, shy girl who had been sent from Florida to live with relatives because her mother didn't think she could take care of her anymore. Catherine knew right away from the look on Jenny's face that she was terrified about coming to a new school where she knew no one and was unfamiliar with the way things were done. Catherine said to Jenny, "Don't worry. This is my first year here, too. We can be new together." This seemed to ease Jenny's mind, and on the first day of school Catherine greeted a little girl whose face radiated eagerness rather than fear.

A few weeks into the school year, a problem arose. It was common practice at Pine Creek to mainstream the self-contained special education students into homerooms, lunch classes, and elective classes. There were several special education students mainstreamed into Catherine's team during lunch; in fact, she had a couple of these students in her lunch class.

There was one child from the emotionally handicapped class who had been placed in Catherine's teammate's class. His name was Marco. Catherine had never had any reason to deal with Marco, but his reputation was enough cause for concern.

On the day of the incident, Catherine's teammate, Mrs. Brooks, was absent from school and a substitute teacher was holding her classes. Everything was going well that day, even lunch seemed to be running smoothly, when Catherine was approached by a distraught Jenny. "What's wrong?" she asked.

"Marco is saying awful things to me, and he won't leave me alone," Jenny replied.

"What sort of things is he saying?" inquired Catherine.

"Bad things that I can't repeat because I'll get into trouble."

Catherine reflected for a moment. She remembered the things she had considered to be bad words when she was in middle school. Was this just a minor dispute? A boy picking on a girl as a means of flirting with her? But if Jenny felt that she couldn't repeat the words, it must be something a little more serious. Perhaps someone should speak to Marco. "I give you my permission to repeat what he said without getting yourself in trouble," Catherine reassured Jenny. Reluctantly, Jenny uttered the words with which Marco had so casually assaulted her.

"He said he was going to f--- me on the lunch table. He said he was going to get his father's handcuffs and chain me to his bed. And when another boy tried to get him to leave me alone, he said, 'You stay out of this, motherf---er.'"

Jenny was on the verge of tears at this point. Catherine was floored. She never expected something like this from a seventh-grader. She knew that something had to be done. It was unsettling for her to realize that the responsibility lay solely on her shoulders since Mrs. Brooks was absent. She decided that she would rather not deal directly with Marco, so she would take it to her administrator.

Catherine told Jenny to move to another lunch table, and she would handle the rest. When she returned to her classroom, she pulled out a discipline slip and wrote down what Jenny had told her. She felt that the situation was serious, and that the principal should be aware of the language that was used to threaten Jenny. She held the discipline slip until the next morning when Mrs. Brooks returned to school. She asked Mrs. Brooks's advice about which of the two of them should handle the situation. Mrs. Brooks deferred to Catherine, saying that Catherine had more direct

Pine Creek Middle School DISCIPLINE NOTICE

Student's Name: *Marco Smith* ☐B ☑W ☐F ☑M

Homeroom: *Marsha Brooks (504)*

Date/Time of Incident: *9/19/98 lunch*

Parents: *Don and Barbara Smith*

Address: *203 N. Cedar Street*

Parent Telephone No. *888-4328*

Grade/Room # *seventh*

RECORD OF INCIDENT   TEACHER ACTION PRIOR TO REFERRAL

Made crude comments to other students   ☐ Conference
(2 girls)"I want to f--- you on the table." ☐ Telephone call(s)
"I will take my dad's handcuffs and hand-   ☐ Detention
cuff you to the bed."Called another male   ☐ Counseling
student a "mother f---er."(Student has a   ☐ Time out/BIR
witness.)   ☐ Other

HAS THE STUDENT BEEN REFERRED TO THE SCHOOL ADMINISTRATOR PRIOR TO THIS INCIDENT?   ☐ Yes   ☐ No

THIS STUDENT HAS BEEN REFERRED FOR DISCIPLINARY ACTION AND THE FOLLOWING ACTIONS HAVE BEEN TAKEN:

_____ A PARENT CONFERENCE AT SCHOOL WILL BE NECESSARY. PLEASE CALL THE OFFICE TO ARRANGE AN APPOINTMENT WITH THE ADMINISTRATOR WHOSE NAME APPEARS BELOW.

Student's Signature   Date   School Administrator   Date knowledge of the events. Mrs. Brooks agreed that it was a very serious infraction that needed immediate attention.

After meeting with Mrs. Brooks, Catherine went directly to Ms. Goodwine. She was in her office. Catherine was relieved that she would not have to place the slip in Ms. Goodwine's box, where it might wait for hours on end. She handed the slip directly to the administrator. Ms. Goodwine took a moment to read the paper. Then she chuckled and said, "Marco wants a girlfriend so badly."

DISCUSSION QUESTIONS

1. What is this case about?
   a. What was the teacher's problem from her point of view?
   b. From your point of view?
2. What do we know about Catherine?
   a What do we know about Catherine's previous teaching experience?
   b. How did Catherine view seventh grade? Do you agree with Catherine's views?
   c. What was Catherine's view of Ms. Goodwine on the first day of school?
3. What do we know about the school community?
   a. How would you describe the school community?
   b. How does the incident of five years ago relate to the current case?
   c. What do we know about the seventh grade?
   d. What do we know about Ms. Goodwine?
4. What do we know about Jenny?
5. Did Catherine and Jenny have a good rapport? What established their rapport? How does this rapport relate to the case?
6. What do we know about Marco?
   a. Was Marco's reputation deserved?
   b. Was Marco a typical seventh-grader?
7. What was the incident in the lunchroom?
   a. How did Catherine handle the incident?
   b. Did Catherine handle the incident properly?
8. What do you think happened after Ms. Goodwine read the discipline slip and told Catherine that Marco wanted a girlfriend?
   a. How do you think Ms. Goodwine dealt with the discipline slip?
   b. What should Catherine have said in response to Ms. Goodwine?

FOR FURTHER REFLECTION

1. Do you think special education students should be mainstreamed into regular classrooms or into regular school events as at Pine Creek?
2. Is Marco a typical special education student? A typical "emotionally handicapped" student?
3. Do you think Marco's behavior would improve or worsen if he were included in more regular school events?
4. What is your philosophy regarding the inclusion of disabled pupils?

FOR SCHOOL LEADERS

1. Which ISLLC standards apply to this case?
2. Is the seventh-grade reputation warranted?
3. Should administrators have special training for middle school?
4. How should Ms. Goodwine deal with Marco? Catherine?

CHAPTER TWO

The Student with the Schedule

PART A

From the moment I looked over my homeroom students' schedules, I knew I was faced with an unusual situation. Jeremy's schedule indicated a bizarre arrangement of classes. He was scheduled for the program for gifted and talented students *and* for compensatory math, a program for those identified as low achievers. He was also scheduled for the special education program, having been identified as learning disabled (LD) and having an attention deficit disorder (ADD). On top of all of this, I immediately noted that Jeremy was scheduled for my advanced English class. In my fifteen years of teaching, I had never seen a schedule like this one!

Two days later, I met "the student with the schedule." Jeremy was a new sixth-grader at Smire Middle School, a suburban school with a student population of approximately nine hundred. Sixth-graders composed approximately one-third of the student body and were distributed among eleven fully certified teachers. Both the student and faculty populations are predominantly white with approximately 35 percent minority. The school is regarded as a cohesive unit, with a minimum of racial problems, and innovative in instruction with achievement above the norm for the district.

When Jeremy walked into class that first day, it was immediately obvious to me that he set his own standards. I knew by his street address that he lived in an upper-middle-class neighborhood, yet he wore baggy, worn shorts, a huge T-shirt that was stretched out of shape, and tattered tennis shoes. His blond hair fell long and straight over his eyes. He appeared unkempt. He was loud and within a few seconds began to make wisecracks about the other students. He conversed boisterously with his friends while I was trying to establish first-day classroom decorum. I spoke to him directly several times, gave him "the look," and finally just told him to be quiet—all to no avail. Homeroom over, he moved on.

"He's taking Ritalin once a day here at school," explained Mrs. Gray, the school nurse. "That's all I know."

Mrs. Gray had overheard me ask the school secretary if we had any information about Jeremy Dunn that I needed before I checked his permanent record.

"Could we double that dose?" I chuckled as I walked away.

Within a few weeks, I realized that Jeremy Dunn was no laughing matter. I realize now, in retrospect, that Jeremy might have fared better in the "current" middle school than the "middle school" of that time. Smire Middle was functioning as a junior high or a "mini–high school." Perhaps within the true middle school concept, a team of teachers could have gotten a handle on the situation much quicker than we did. Unfortunately, communication broke down. Although there was consensus among all of Jeremy's teachers that we had major problems, we never seemed to be able to get together to hash out possible solutions.

Middle School Concept

The primary distinguishing feature of the "current" middle school is its student-centeredness. Rather than focusing on courses or subjects, the middle school concept is founded on its focus on students. The middle school concept is based on an awareness and responsiveness to the developmental needs—cognitive, physical, emotional, social—of students in transescence. The organization of the school, the curriculum, instruction, and support services are all constructed in such a way as to address and support middle-level-aged students.

Jeremy could not keep pace academically in my advanced English class. He didn't know a complete sentence from a fragment, nor a verb from a noun. I was familiar with his elementary school and stunned by his lack of preparation. His poor skills only contributed to his misbehavior in the classroom.

If I said to the class, "Take out your textbook," he shouted, "Why?"

If I said to the class, "Let's look at these sentences," he blared, "I can't see!"

If I said to the class, "Tom, give me a example of a run-on sentence," he blurted, "Diarrhea!"

PART B

The teachers' lounge was crowded, and I had an important phone call to make. Sometimes, it's difficult to hear; besides, I'm not sure I wanted everyone to hear this call. We'd only been in school a few days and Jeremy had been chronically problematic. So far he had completed none of his work. He talks out in class, makes smart remarks . . .

"I just pulled his permanent folder." Interrupted from my thoughts, I realized that Mrs. Brown, another one of Jeremy's teachers, was talking to me. "Look at this."

What a surprise it was to me as we studied Jeremy's cumulative school record. The amazement registered on both of our faces as we discovered that each year, without a doubt, Jeremy had failed every subject. Yet, each year—recorded permanently, in black and white—this kid had been placed in the next grade. He had never attended summer school or any special program.

"I can't believe it," I spoke quietly.

"Can't believe what?" came a query from another teacher who had overheard my remark.

"Jeremy Dunn has been placed every year since first grade, yet his grades were always failing," I explained, not feeling at all calm.

I had a problem. We had a problem. We wanted to work to solve this problem. Because Jeremy was such a contradiction and his behavior was so aberrant, Mrs. Brown and I were determined to find a way to support him and one another. A review of his file from the previous school indicated that Jeremy historically had been unsuccessful in school, yet there appeared to be no "recipe" for a "cure." He had never actually "passed" or been promoted from grade to grade in elementary school, but each year had been "placed" in the next grade.

PART C

I made that phone call, but rather than discuss the issues over the telephone, I arranged for a conference. The conference was scheduled to include all of Jeremy's teachers, both parents, and the principal. Jeremy was invited at his mother's request.

I have never, prior to or since this conference, been witness to such disrespect as shown by Jeremy to his mother. Jeremy's father did not attend the conference. In the conference, Jeremy was sullen. He slouched in his seat, hiding behind his hair. I had only previously witnessed the animated, vocal Jeremy. This was a different child. When his mother asked him to sit up, he either said no or completely ignored her.

"I will not continue in this conference if Jeremy cannot sit up, participate, and treat his mother with respect." I heard these words come out of me, and I couldn't believe it. I was so angry that this eleven-year-old child's mother was allowing him to treat her this way. In addition, I felt nothing could be resolved in this atmosphere. But I was still shocked at my own response.

As problems and solutions were discussed, Jeremy's mother appeared to understand and accept them. She agreed to a plan that included maintaining a homework notebook and arranging for after-school tutoring. She indicated that there would be strong support from home with supervision and follow-up.

"We always check behind Jeremy and try to help him stay organized. We check to see that his assignments are completed. It will be easier if we have a homework notebook signed by everyone, and the after-school tutoring should help, too." Mrs. Dunn spoke convincingly. Jeremy chuckled derisively and shook his head. He clearly didn't believe one word she said. She alternately ignored him and apologized for him throughout the conference.

PART D

I learned a great deal that day. In addition to my observations of the parent-child interaction, I learned a new fact: Jeremy's mother was the chairperson of the constituent school board that supervised our school. The county school district is large and consolidated, so that smaller, constituent school districts, with elected boards and assigned superintendents, have been constituted to deal with local transportation and discipline matters.

As the school year progressed, Jeremy's behavior and academic problems continued. There were brief periods of cooperation in various classes, but Jeremy's academic deficiencies made success unfamiliar to him. More conferences were held—all the same and to no avail. Jeremy's father never attended. His mother was generally agreeable, always pledging more support from home. Never, in any conference, was Jeremy pleasant or polite to his mother. During one of these conferences later in the year, Jeremy's mother agreed that he should be retained in sixth grade based on his progress reports, barring drastic academic improvements on his part.

Near the end of the last quarter of school, it was clear that Jeremy would not meet the requirements for promotion so another conference was scheduled. The final conference never took place. Jeremy's mother met privately with the constituent district superintendent, and then with the superintendent and our school principal. She stated that she could not allow Jeremy to repeat sixth grade. The emotional and social stigmatization would be too overwhelming for Jeremy because of his disabilities. The damage would be irreparable. Jeremy was placed in seventh grade the following year.

DISCUSSION QUESTIONS FOR PART A

1. What is this case about?
   a. What was the teacher's problem from her point of view? From your point of view?
   b. What should the teacher do next?
2. What do we know about Jeremy?
   a. How would you describe Jeremy?
   b. What is his grade level? What kinds of problems might this introduce?
   c. How does Jeremy mesh with the school and student characteristics at Smire Middle School?
3. What do we know about the teacher?
   a. How would you describe the teacher?
   b. What role does the teacher's experience play in this case?
   c. Does the teacher exhibit any biases? Toward Jeremy?
4. Do you consider Jeremy to be a discipline problem? What alternative strategies could be employed?
5. What is the "look"? Is it a useful attribute to cultivate? Why?
6. Why might Jeremy have fared better under the current middle school concept?
7. Are there implications in this case for a school uniform or dress code policy? What are the pros and cons of such policies for middle-level students?

DISCUSSION QUESTIONS FOR PART B

1. What is this case about?
   a. What was the teacher's problem from her point of view? From your point of view?
   b. What should the teacher do next?
   c. What was the important phone call the teacher had to make?
2. Did the teacher gather adequate information to solve the problem?
   a. What kind of information did the teacher gather?
   b. What is a cumulative school record? What information did it provide?
   c. How does placement differ from promotion?
3. Would you describe the teacher as student-centered?
4. Has your assessment of Jeremy changed? Your assessment of the teacher?

DISCUSSION QUESTIONS FOR PART C

1. Did the teacher solve the problem by scheduling a conference?
   a. Was a conference an appropriate approach to solving the problem?
   b. Were the appropriate participants invited?
   c. Should Jeremy have been included?
   d. What was the outcome of the conference?
2. Describe the relationship between Jeremy and his mother?
   a. What impact do you think this relationship had on Jeremy's school performance?
   b. How could school personnel use this information in planning for Jeremy?
   c. Do you think the teacher was right to be "shocked at my own response"?
3. What was the plan? What is your assessment of the plan? Alternative strategies?
4. How should a parent-teacher conference be organized?

DISCUSSION QUESTIONS FOR PART D

1. What new information did the teacher learn in the conference?
   a. What impact did this information have on the case?

   b. Was Jeremy's mother's position a deterrent or a help to his school welfare?

2. Was the case solved appropriately?
3. Did the parent act in the best interests of the child? The superintendent? The principal?
4. What alternative strategies could have been employed by school personnel to solve this problem differently?
5. How do you think the teacher felt at the end of this case?

FOR FURTHER REFLECTION

1. What was the teacher's gender? What affect did gender play in this case?
2. What was the father's role in the case? Could alternative strategies be employed to change the father's role?
3. Would you describe the teacher as a behaviorist, a developmentalist, a humanist?

FOR SCHOOL LEADERS

1. Which ISLLC standards apply to this case?
2. What role did politics play in this case? Is it possible for an administrator to adequately balance politics with a child's welfare in a case like this one?
3. Could the principal have better prepared the teachers for the outcome of this case?

CHAPTER THREE

Cases within Cases

Sis Kind, a well-liked professor at Local Military University (LMU), did not know what to do. She was afraid that she had insulted Kate Braden, an excellent language arts teacher in her Middle School Project.

The Middle School Project was a special program that Sis had developed over the past two years. It had been difficult to gain the acceptance of her department chair because the state did not offer middle school certification and he was dedicated to the secondary education degree. The program had finally been funded by a one-time LMU grant, and Kate had been instrumental in attracting teachers to participate.

Kate had previously had an unfortunate experience with a student teacher assigned to her supervision. As a result, she thought that it was imperative for future teachers to have more field experiences prior to student teaching, and for teachers assigned to middle schools to have specialized training. The program that Sis proposed included these important features so when Sis approached her about the program, Kate hardly thought twice before deciding to participate.

The Middle School Project proposed by Sis was a three-phase program. In the first phase, middle school teachers would participate in a course, "Reflective Practice in the Middle School," which would be offered in a shortened summer school format. The course would require reflection on one's practice and would familiarize participants with case-based instruction. As part of the course, the participants would write a case about a dilemma they faced as a middle school teacher.

In the second phase, course participants would become co-professors for a "Methods and Materials" course offered to Masters in Teaching (MAT) students during the fall term. As co-professors, each participant would be responsible for one (or possibly two) class meeting in which he or she would instruct from cases developed during the summer course.

The teachers would also function as mentors/contacts for the MAT students who would be required to observe/assist in classrooms.

During the spring semester, the MAT students would be placed in the participants' schools for professional internship. Although each teacher/participant/co-professor might not supervise a student teacher, they would function as a supportive nucleus to assist the MAT students throughout this phase. Each participant would receive a voucher for a course for his or her role as part of the supervising team.

Sis and Kate had known each other for years. They had worked on a school-based management team at Ashley Middle School, the school where Kate taught before coming to Pinckney Middle School. Sis had been employed in the office of research for the school district and served as evaluator for the Ashley team. The two women had a good rapport and a mutual respect for each other. Thus, it was natural that Sis had chosen Kate for the first class presentation of her case.

Kate's case was about a student with a variety of disabilities and a mother on the local school board. During earlier brainstorming sessions, Kate was so animated when she spoke about the case. It came alive. She shared her anger and her frustration. The other teachers in the discussion circle felt her emotions when she spoke.

"A couple of days after the beginning of school, the school secretary showed me Jeremy's perm[anent] folder. I was shocked. Every year, he had failed. Failed every subject. But every year, he was placed in the next grade. He didn't even go to summer school."

Kate had explained how surprised she was to have Jeremy in her advanced English class while he was also enrolled in a remedial class for math, a special education pull-out class, and a class for gifted and talented students. Having formerly been a special education teacher, Kate was not unfamiliar with learning disabilities or attention deficit disorder. It was just, as she said to the others, "In fifteen years of teaching I had never seen a schedule like that." Kate explained, "He just couldn't keep up in class. He didn't know a complete sentence from a fragment. He didn't have the English skills so he began to act out in class." Kate hypothesized that if her school had been a "middle school" in concept at the time of Jeremy's case, it might never have become a case: "At that time, we were called a middle school, but we functioned like a junior high school."

All of the other teachers in the class were spellbound and outraged. Kate was such an energetic and dedicated educator. It was obvious that she was an outstanding teacher. The less experienced teachers from Crestlake had already garnered lots of good ideas from Kate. Even the other teachers from Pinckney who were familiar with Kate's story were totally engrossed by her storytelling manner.

Sis was especially pleased at how well the teachers from the three different schools had bonded. In addition to Kate, there were two other teachers from Pinckney Middle School, a school that had established a positive reputation for being innovative. The "top-ten teachers," as the class became known, also included one teacher from Hillville Middle School and six teachers from Crestlake Middle School. Nine of the ten teachers were female, and all were white. Prior to the class, the teachers from the different schools were strangers to one another. The teachers from Crestlake were generally "more junior" than the teachers from the other schools. In fact, one of the teachers from Pinckney had taught junior high school when Bill, the only male and a first-year teacher, had been enrolled as a student.

But they all took note when Kate spat out, "I was so mad, I could have slapped him." The climax of Jeremy's case was a parent-teacher conference with he and his mother present. Jeremy treated his mother with obvious contempt, a trait Kate could not abide in an eleven-year-old child.

When Kate told her story, it sparked a discussion about how teachers did not like all students. Jean, an experienced teacher from Hillville, thought that future teachers ought to be aware of their own humanness. She wanted to apprise them of "the bad as well as the good." Mindy and Bill, Crestlake teachers, outspokenly defended the teacher's right to his or her own feelings as long as they acted "professionally" toward all students.

Today, several days after the brainstorming session, rough drafts of all cases had been due. The cases were circulated for editing and critique. After sitting and reading for a couple of hours, the teachers were getting restless and urged Sis to convene the discussion circle.

Sis was uncertain how to proceed. She wanted to be sure that a sufficient number of teachers had read each case so that the critique session would be meaningful. Some of the cases were not well written. Sis found herself wishing that she had enrolled in the school district's Writing Project, where teachers wrote and shared and critiqued each other's writing. She had heard positive comments about the project. It certainly would help her to know how to proceed now.

Kate was vocal: "Come on. Let's just discuss the cases. We're ready." Sis thought about Kate's case. It was well written, but it was sterile. It was stripped of all of those wonderful emotions that Kate expressed when she talked about the case. It was written in third person and impersonal. The first line read, "Note a student schedule with the following classes: gifted and talented, compensatory math, special education, advanced English."

"Come on," Kate urged. Sis hesitated for a moment. Where to begin? Kate was a strong teacher. She taught language arts. She had probably been a part of the Writing Project. She was probably used to having her writing critiqued. And her case was so good, fundamentally. It just needed to be expressed the same way it had been presented orally. Sis took a deep breath and started with Kate's case.

"Kate, your case is so good, but I think you need to put some emotion into it."

Did Kate blanch when she said that?

Kate countered, "But I didn't think we should put our point of view into it. I thought we should be objective and let the students decide what they thought about it. I didn't think I should let them know what I was thinking. They should learn from it—make up their own minds."

"I think it would be more readable if you expressed your feelings. You know, something like 'Imagine how surprised I was to see a schedule which included . . .' Sort of like that case that we read where the teacher cried through her class."

"But I didn't think there was a particular style that we had to use when we wrote our cases."

Bill joined the discussion. "Well, when I was at Longbranch College, we had a great teacher education program. We used cases a lot. I really think it was helpful to know what the teacher thought and felt."

The discussion didn't end there. In fact it went on for the remainder of the class period. Kate spoke about how meaningful it was for her to be a teacher. Sis could hear tears in her voice. What damage had she done? Could it be repaired? How?

DISCUSSION QUESTIONS

1. What is this case about?
2. What do we know about the professor?
3. What do we know about Kate?
4. What do we know about the relationship between the professor and Kate?
5. What do we know about the other participants? What do we know about the interrelationships in the group?

6. Is there a right or better way to write a case?
   a. Should a case be written in first or third person? Why?
   b. Should a case be written subjectively or objectively? Why?
   c. Should a case include the teacher's emotions and feelings even if they are not "socially appropriate"? What is the impact of a line like "I was so mad, I could have slapped him"?
7. What do you think of Jean's viewpoint that teachers ought to be made aware of their own humanness? That teachers should know about "the bad as well as the good" in the profession?
8. What do you think of Mindy and Bill's position that teachers are entitled to their feelings about students as long as they act "professionally" toward all students?
9. Why was Kate upset? Why was Sis upset?
10. Was any "damage done"? If so, how could it be repaired?

FOR FURTHER REFLECTION

1. Should states require or offer middle-level certification? Why or why not?
2. Should colleges and universities provide special training programs for middle-level teachers? Why or why not?
3. What aspects of this case could be generalized to a middle school classroom situation?
4. How are middle school teachers like and unlike middle school pupils?
5. Of what value would case writing be to middle school teachers? Should it be approached as an individual activity or should it be structured as a group activity? How would you structure such an activity?

FOR SCHOOL LEADERS

1. Which ISLLC standards apply to this case?
2. Would you welcome the opportunity for your school to be involved in a project like the Middle School Project? Why or why not?
3. How can the school administrator facilitate the development of new professionals? The development of practicing educators?
4. Can you see a way of incorporating case writing and discussion groups into your faculty development program? What would be the pros and cons?

CHAPTER FOUR

Ghost Story

The note read, "Please call me at your earliest convenience."

As an almost twenty-year veteran teacher, this note did not unduly concern me. I did observe, however, that the handwritten words were on legal stationery. Judging from the letterhead and signature, the mother of one of my seventh-grade advanced English students wanted to discuss something with me and had chosen a piece of her attorney-husband's office stationery. Yet, this did not forewarn me of what was to come.

Having taught English to seventh-graders in this affluent, suburban middle school for three years after a background of teaching high school English for fourteen years, I found nothing in my experience to cause alarm. However, as a "rule of thumb," before calling parents, I always review my recent experiences with their child (in this case, Bill) and the class content.

Bill's grades were passable but not excellent. He usually averaged low "B" work. He and I had had no conflicts; as a matter of fact, I found him to be pleasant and to display a positive attitude in class. To continue my preparation for the return phone call, I contemplated what we were covering in class. We were immersed in something the students really enjoyed. Rather than having my students write a topic paper that required research, I had stumbled across an idea the year before that had been a great success. My students wrote short stories that were set in the Beaufort area prior to 1900. To do this effectively, they researched the history of Beaufort, chose a specific time period, and wrote their stories blending the facts of time with their fiction. In other words, they wrote a historical fiction. My students from last year had enjoyed writing and learning about the history of the community so much that I had decided to use the same assignment again.

Last year, I had assisted my students by reading them a ghost story set in Beaufort at the time of the American Revolutionary War. The students loved the story and begged me to take them to see the actual house in which the story was set. They bombarded me with "Please take us to see the house," and "Our papers would be so much better if we could tour the historic district." The pleading was incessant, so after much planning, I organized a field trip that consisted of a walking tour of the homes of Beaufort in which ghost stories were purportedly set.

Permission letters for parents had resulted in an overwhelming response. My explanation of the purpose and plans for the trip had elicited more parent volunteers to chaperone than I could ever accommodate. Other parents sent notes praising the idea. The actual field trip during the spring of the previous year had been an enormous success. The students learned a lot of relevant information that appeared in their stories.

I had made two modifications to the trip for this year, the trip that Bill and his classmates were soon to embark upon. I had decided to teach this unit in the fall and planned a field trip or "ghostwalk" for ten days before Halloween. Permission slips had been received by parents only a few days before Bill's mother wrote to me. Once again, I was receiving many requests to chaperone and numerous complimentary notes. Bill had not returned his permission form, so I assumed that his mother wanted to talk to me about the trip. I was right about that, but I never once guessed the exact nature of our conversation.

"Bill, do you know what your mom wants to talk to me about?" I asked innocently when we unexpectedly met in the media center.

"I don't know," he stammered, head down.

This demeanor was not typical of Bill. He must be in trouble with his parents, I thought nonchalantly.

I called Bill's mother, Mrs. Smith, the same night I received the note. I was prepared. She was extremely cordial in her greeting and then came directly to the point.

"Mrs. Jones," she intoned pleasantly, "my husband and I have read your letter concerning the tour of Beaufort and your reading of some ghost stories, and we cannot approve of this. According to the Bible, ghosts do not exist, and we do not want our son exposed to such literature."

I was shocked. Nothing in my background had prepared me for this. I consider myself to be religious, yet I could not understand her reasoning.

"Mrs. Smith, I don't believe in ghosts either. This is one genre of literature that I read to my students," I managed to respond.

After my response, I received what amounted to a biblical lesson on ghosts. Mrs. Smith was extremely nice to me as she spoke, even complimenting my teaching, but she continually reiterated that she could not support this field trip. I offered an accommodation for Bill, allowing him to work on his short story in the media center in lieu of the field trip. Mrs. Smith accepted my suggestion and closed our conversation with a prayer.

My classes participated in the field trip and both students and parent-chaperones seemed to benefit from it. No other complaints were received, only compliments. But the trip was ruined for me. I was so self-conscious and paranoid as I read the final paragraphs of each story on site at the historical location where some innocuous ghost would appear that the joy of this trip was lost forever with me.

In the weeks following the trip, I consulted with my own Lutheran pastor. I also spoke with an Episcopal priest and a Methodist minister. None of these clerics expressed any concerns about the ghostwalk.

While I still conduct a historical tour of Beaufort, I do not call it a ghostwalk and the word "ghosts" appears neither in the permission letter nor in the stories I read. I edit all of the stories to have a different plot or resolution. The emphases of the current trip are the architecture of the various historical periods, historical facts, and local color of the stories. It has grown into an interdisciplinary unit for our teaching/learning team. In many ways, the unit has been improved and expanded, but in my opinion, the luster of the first trip has been lost forever.

Interdisciplinary Unit

A unit or instructional program that integrates subject matter from several different disciplines. Rather than each subject being taught separately, subjects like history, literature, science, and mathematics are all focused on the same thematic unit and taught around that unit.

DISCUSSION QUESTIONS

1. What is this case about?
2. What do we know about the teacher?
   a. Describe the teacher's background.
   b. What do you think about the teacher's "rule of thumb" before calling parents?

  c. What is your view of the way in which the teacher conducted the telephone conversation with Mrs. Smith? What suggestions do you have?
3. What do we know about Bill and the Smith family?
  a. How would you characterize Bill as a student?
  b. Describe Bill's parents.
4. What is your view of the teacher's lesson and field trip? Do you believe that the teacher should have changed her field trip in future years?
5. How will this case affect your experience as a teacher?

FOR FURTHER REFLECTION

1. What is an interdisciplinary unit? How would an interdisciplinary unit improve the Beaufort field trip? Which disciplines should be involved? Can you think of a few sample activities?
2. What are some differences in teaching high school and middle school? Can a high school teacher make a successful transition to middle school? Can a middle school teacher make a successful transition to high school?

FOR SCHOOL LEADERS

1. Which ISLLC standards apply to this case?
2. How knowledgeable should the principal be about individual teachers' class activities?
3. Before reading this case, what would your response have been about the teacher's planned activities? After reading the case?

CHAPTER FIVE

The Challenge

I thought that the ghostwalk would be the challenge of my career, but Bill and his family continued to haunt me. After winter break (certainly not to be called "Christmas vacation"), I returned to school refreshed. The lessons of the "Ghost Story" had not been forgotten, but they were not an ever-present concern. A new year and a new semester brought a refreshed attitude for me and the students.

The district office had provided class sets of a science fiction novel that had been selected for all middle schools. I assigned the novel, which we began to read and discuss in class. After a week, I announced a quiz for the following Friday. On Thursday, I received a note from Bill's mother. Again, it was handwritten on legal stationery. Its contents requested that I call to discuss the novel.

After the earlier incident, I anticipated a religious challenge to the book. I carefully reviewed the recommended book list for the district and identified several alternatives. I notified my principal about the note. I had done my homework and was prepared for the telephone conversation, yet I felt unsettled as I dialed the Smith residence.

Mrs. Smith answered. As anticipated, she expressed disapproval of science fiction on religious grounds. "Bill is upset about having to read this novel," Mrs. Smith intoned. "It is offensive to him. It is in opposition to our religious beliefs."

"Mrs. Smith, I will be happy to provide a copy of the district book list to you. You can select another book for Bill to read. The book we are reading now was assigned two weeks ago and a test is scheduled for tomorrow, but I would be happy to make an accommodation for him."

"I'll think about your offer, Mrs. Jones," she replied and continued, "Science fiction is just not something we can approve of . . . it defies our religion. All fantasy is against our beliefs."

"Well, Mrs. Smith, the very first story in our literature book was 'Riki Tiki Tavi.' If you recall, the story is about a mongoose that talks. And that is certainly fantasy. Do you object to the entire literature book?"

Mrs. Smith gave no response. But the next day, I received another hand-written note from her on legal stationery. It read, "I don't want Bill to be 'punished' by reading another book. There is no reason for him to be sin-gled out or have to feel different from other students. I don't want *any* stu-dent to be forced to read this book."

After consulting with my principal, I compiled a package for Mrs. Smith and sent it to her. The package contained the procedures for for-mally challenging a book or curricular practice. Mrs. Smith took action. After scheduling a meeting with the principal and me, she completed the "Request for Reconsideration of Instructional Material." In line with the procedures outlined in the district policy, I began to complete the "In-structional Objectives and Specific Values of Instructional Materials."

I busily prepared for this meeting. I was required to acquire book re-views on the novel and present them at the meeting. I was more dogged in my library work than I had ever been in preparing papers for my own graduate classes. I found as much material as I could on the novel.

My biggest disappointment occurred when I called the district office and spoke to the language arts coordinator, Becky O'Dowd. She and I had an excellent relationship. I had served on a number of district committees. I had even taught one of her children. I explained the situation to Becky and requested documentation of suggestion of the book for reading by middle school students. Then I asked Becky to attend the meeting with the Smiths.

"Liza," she explained gently, "I can't attend the meeting."

I interrupted, "But I really need your support. I need for you to explain how this book was selected and to tell them that all of the middle schools are using it."

She replied, "I *am not allowed* to attend by district policy. If you and the parents don't reach an agreement, they can appeal to the superinten-dent. Then a committee will be assigned and I will automatically be a mem-ber. I'm sorry, Liza, but I will send you the memoranda about the book."

We closed the conversation with Becky wishing me well, but I couldn't help thinking that it was her job to serve teachers. I felt attacked by the parents and unsupported by my coordinator. The principal was going to depend on me to justify the selection of the book. It was going to be me against the Smiths.

Both Mr. and Mrs. Smith attended the meeting. Mrs. Smith opened by describing how Bill had come to her and said, "Mom, I just can't read the book we've been assigned. It goes against everything I believe." My prin-

⬧School District   POLICY #1001

Reconsideration of Instructional Materials   Page 2 of 5

Procedure of Requesting Withdrawal of Educational Materials

A. The question concerning the material must be presented by a parent or guardian of a student in the classroom where the material was used or made available.

B. The parent must contact the teacher involved and/or the principal. If the parent contacts the teacher, the teacher should immediately notify the principal. If the parent contacts any other school official, the parent must be directed to the principal to schedule an appointment.

C. The principal should assure the parent that the parent's opinion will be considered and his/her interest is welcome. The principal must inform the parent and the teacher of the procedure to be followed. No discussion of the material is to take place prior to the established conference where parent, teacher, and principal are all present.

D. At least twenty-four hours prior to the conference, the parent or guardian must return to the principal of the school two copies of the completed form entitled, "Request for Reconsideration of Educational Material." At least twenty-four hours prior to the conference, the teacher must submit to the principal two copies of the completed form entitled, "Instructional Objectives and Specific Values of Educational Materials." The principal should give a copy of the request for withdrawal of the material to the teacher and a copy of the instructional objectives and specific values of materials to the parent.

E. During the conference, the principal shall assist the teacher and parent in their attempts to reach a decision agreeable to both.

F. If, after the conference, the parent would like to pursue the request for withdrawal, the principal will direct the parent to mail copies of the original request to the School District Superintendent and the Deputy Superintendent for Instruction. The teacher must send copies of the instructional objectives and specific values to the School District Superintendent and the Deputy Superintendent for Instruction. These forms are to be mailed no later than five calendar days following the conference. The use of challenged materials shall not be restricted until final disposition, but individuals may be excused from using challenged materials.

✏️**School District**	POLICY #1001
Reconsideration of Instructional Materials	Page 3 of 5

G. The material will be reviewed again in light of the objections raised. This reviewing shall be done within twenty (20) school days after the material has been questioned. A definite procedure will be followed to ensure that the incident is given due importance and treated objectively and unemotionally.

  1. A committee to review the material shall be appointed by the Deputy Superintendent for Instruction who shall serve and act as chairperson. In addition, it shall contain:

    a. Coordinator of the discipline areas involved.

    b. Two teachers in the discipline area involved but from a school other than the one in the original dispute.

    c. A principal in a school other than the one in the original dispute.

    d. Two parents from different school attendance areas than the one involved in the dispute.

  2. Within the twenty school days, the committee shall study all materials and forms referred to it and submit its recommendation to the District Superintendent in writing.

H. After studying the recommendation of the committee, the District Superintendent shall make his/her decision and forward a copy to the parent involved. If the recommendation is not satisfactory to the parent, the District Superintendent will present the recommendation to the School Board for final action at the next regular meeting.

I. The parent, teacher, and principal originally involved shall be notified in writing of the Board's decision.

The request of withdrawal of educational materials may be dropped at any time the parent so desires.

REQUEST FOR RECONSIDERATION
OF INSTRUCTIONAL MATERIAL

This form is to be completed in duplicate and returned to the principal at least 24 hours prior to your conference with the principal and teacher.

TYPE OF MATERIAL: _____

TITLE: _____

AUTHOR, EDITOR, PUBLISHER: _____

_____

YOUR NAME: _____ HOME TELEPHONE: _____

ADDRESS: _____ OFFICE TELEPHONE: _____

1. Did you read or study the entire body of material? _____

2. What, specifically, do you find objectionable in the use of this material?
   a. _____
   b. _____
   c. _____

3. What do you feel might be the result of using this material?
   a. _____
   b. _____
   c. _____

4. Do you think this material is available to the student outside of the classroom? If so, where? _____

5. What do you believe is the theme of this material?

   _____

6. What good points are there in this material?
   a. _____
   b. _____
   c. _____

7. For what age group would you recommend this material? _____

8. Are you aware of the judgment of this material by recognized critics? _____

9. In its place, what material of equal value would you recommend that would give as valuable a picture and perspective of societies? ____

   _____

Signature: _____ Date: _____

INSTRUCTIONAL OBJECTIVES AND SPECIFIC
VALUES OF INSTRUCTIONAL MATERIALS

This form is to be filled out completely in duplicate and returned to the principal at least twenty-four hours prior to your conference with the principal and the parent with a request for reconsideration of materials.

TYPES OF MATERIAL: _____

AUTHOR, EDITOR, PUBLISHER: _____

_____

YOUR NAME: _____

SCHOOL: _____

1. List your instructional objectives connected to the use of the questioned material.

    a. _____
    _____

    b. _____
    _____

    c. _____
    _____

2. List specific values in using this material to develop your objectives.

    a. _____
    _____

    b. _____
    _____

    c. _____
    _____

What is the judgment of this material by recognized critics? (Include examples of conflicting reviews, if available.) _____

_____
_____
_____
_____

cipal asked her to elaborate and she said, "We don't believe in science fiction. Fantasy is contrary to our religious beliefs."

I once again reiterated my points about "Riki Tiki Tavi" and the literature book, but this time I went a little further to explain that it was taken from *The Jungle Book* by Rudyard Kipling, a Nobel Prize winner. I then explained how the science fiction novel had been selected by the district and supplied to all district middle schools. I described how my own children had read and enjoyed the science fiction story when they had been middle-schoolers. I tried to place it in the genres of literature and quickly summarized the positive reviews it had received.

Mrs. Smith was patient, but when I finished, she stated: "I have read the book and on page fifty-two it has objectionable language."

I was prepared for this. "The word (I pointed to the "damn" on page fifty-two for my principal) is only used once in the entire book. And no other words like that are used. It is used to belittle the character that uses it. It is one method of characterization." I then spoke about Huck Finn and how sometimes his character was misunderstood. "Huck was ridiculing slavery, not upholding it," I concluded.

I paused. I felt I had been more eloquent than usual in my explanations. The preparation and the adrenaline of fear, I thought, had served me well.

Mr. Smith broke the silence. He had not spoken throughout the meeting, and he had not been involved in the earlier field trip incident. "How many book challenges has this book had? I don't mean just at this school or in the district. I mean how often has it been challenged ever?"

"None. It has never been challenged before."

Mr. Smith considered my answer and said, "I think we will withdraw our challenge. However, we don't want our son to read this book."

The remainder of the meeting was spent shaping an agreement by which Bill and the Smiths would select all of his future reading materials. Every book that Bill read for the remainder of that year was religious in nature.

DISCUSSION QUESTIONS

1. What is this case about?
2. What do you think Bill's motivation was in objecting to the material?
3. Why do you think Mrs. Smith wrote notes on her husband's business stationery?
4. What do we know about the teacher's predisposition toward the parents? Was her knowledge of the family a help or a hindrance?

5. How should one screen the material one uses in class?
   a. How could this incident generalize to other classes (e.g., science and social studies)?
   b. Should genres, theories, and so forth be avoided if they are potentially controversial?
6. Was the parents' decision fair to Bill as a learner?
7. How will this case affect your experience as a teacher?

FOR FURTHER REFLECTION

1. What are some differences in teaching high school and middle school? Can a high school teacher make a successful transition to middle school? Can a middle school teacher make a successful transition to high school?
2. What is the role of district support staff?
3. Whose responsibility is it to set curricula?

FOR SCHOOL LEADERS

1. Which ISLLC standards apply to this case?
2. Based on the previous experience with the parents in this case, would you have monitored the teacher's activities more closely?
3. What is the administrator's role in a situation/meeting like the one described in this case?

CHAPTER SIX

The Test

As I rounded the corner to the school office, the increased noise level assaulted my senses. Then, I spied Dee. He was sitting amid the talking teachers, the ringing telephones, the rushing administrators, *and* he was finishing his test. In this zoo, how could he concentrate? Dee was my student and I had been advised to send him to the office to complete his standardized test. Was this really the appropriate place for him to be? Had I done what was best for Dee, or had I ruined his chance for success?

Standardized Test

A standardized test is one for which testing conditions are held constant. All examinees receive the same instructions and testing conditions. Often, but not always, the test questions are standardized too.

I was in my second year of teaching eighth grade at Pine Middle School. Our school had a good reputation. Of the three middle schools in the district, ours was considered to be the best. Although we had experienced some overcrowding, the school year had gone well.

A few weeks earlier, I had attended a training session for administering the State Assessment Program (SAP). Schools in our state are required to administer SAP, a criterion-referenced achievement test, to sixth- and eighth-graders during the spring of the year. SAP is used as one determinant in promotion decisions at all grade levels, but at the eighth-grade level it is especially important since it is used to set a student's curriculum for high school.

During the training session, the guidance counselor emphasized two things: first, teachers were not to assist students with the test *in any way*,

Criterion-Referenced Test

A criterion-referenced test (CRT) is one in which the scores derive meaning by comparing the examinees to the test content. They are designed to reflect how much (and or what portions) of the curriculum a student has mastered. Oftentimes, CRTs have standards of appropriate performance associated with the scores. If a student reaches a certain score, she or he has met the standard. Otherwise, he or she has not.

Norm-Referenced Test

A norm-referenced test (NRT) is one in which the scores derive meaning by comparison with scores of other examinees. The percentile rank is the quintessential NRT score. A percentile rank of 75 indicates that the examinee has scored above 75 percent of the examinees in the norm group. An important point to remember is that the norm group may be fixed in time (i.e., those tested in 1996) and may not include current examinees.

and second, teachers were not to leave students unattended while they were testing. The guidance counselor reminded us that violating these guidelines could result in investigation by the state law enforcement division and/or dismissal. A teacher could even lose his or her teaching credential! I was extremely nervous about administering the test properly. I loved teaching and did not want to risk my career.

As the first day of testing neared, I role-played situations in my head. I brainstormed possible solutions. I reread the instructor's manual to refresh my memory about testing procedures. Monday morning arrived and I felt prepared, confident, and comfortable about administering the test.

When testing time began, my sixteen students were attentive. They were ready to have testing behind them, too. I distributed test materials, read the instructions aloud, and the students began to work. SAP is known as an "untimed" test, so the students each began to work diligently at his or her own pace. I monitored their work and all students appeared to be concentrating, working steadily, and trying hard. Time passed. A few students completed the test and remained quiet in their seats. More students finished, and all was well. I began to notice teachers passing through the hall carrying test materials. That meant that their classes were finished. More of my students finished the test, and more teachers passed through the hall, and a group of students and teachers began to congregate in the hall.

Only one of my students was still working. His pace did not alarm me because Dee had been diagnosed with learning disabilities and habitually worked at a slower pace than the other students. His Individual Education Plan (IEP) prescribed increased time to complete class work and classroom tests. Under the circumstances, I considered all to be well.

As time passed, however, the other students began to become restless. Those who had been napping woke up; those who had been reading put their books away; those who had been doing nothing metamorphosed from bored to aggravated and impatient. Students began communicating by silently "mouthing" words to each other. In an endeavor to maintain a proper testing environment, I gave them the "eye." Keeping fifteen eighth-graders orderly and occupied while maintaining silence is no easy task!

Another teacher peered through the window in the classroom door and mouthed "Are you finished?" I shook my head no, and turned to observe the class. Dee had been working for about thirty minutes past the last completing student, so I walked over to his desk to try to determine how much more time he would need. As I nonchalantly glanced at his answer sheet, I discovered that he was only halfway through the items. Another glance at the hall confirmed that all of the other teachers were finished with testing. I could discern the growing impatience on their faces. I began to feel panicky. It would take Dee at least another hour to complete his test. Other than my class, the entire grade was finished. The teachers on the other side of the door looked at me as if to say, "You idiot—what's going on?" I had to let them know what was happening.

In contemplating communication with them, the guidelines for administration and the consequences of violating the guidelines raced through my consciousness. Additionally, I did not want to embarrass Dee or force him to rush through the test. I decided to write a note and slip it under the door to the other teachers. When they read it, the teachers nodded in understanding and dispersed.

Suddenly, the assistant principal burst into the classroom and loudly announced, "What is going on here?" The shock on top of my earlier panic rattled me. The intrusion was not good for me or the students. I had to maintain a proper testing environment for Dee. I politely asked the principal to step outside the door to discuss the situation. However, rules in mind, I remained just inside the door so the students would not be unattended with test materials.

A few minutes after the assistant principal left, the guidance counselor arrived. She took Dee's test and escorted him to the office. I thought I had solved the problem appropriately. But when I entered the office and saw Dee, I began to have doubts.

DISCUSSION QUESTIONS

1. What is this case about?
   a. What was the teacher's problem from her point of view?
   b. From your point of view?
2. What do we know about the teacher?
   a. What do we know about the teacher's teaching experience?
   b. How did the teacher view her responsibilities for testing? Do you agree with her views?
3. What do we know about the school?
   a. How did the teacher describe the school?
   b. How does the school community view the importance of testing? Explain your reasoning.
   c. How do the school's views about testing affect the teacher's views? Explain.
4. What do we know about the test?
   a. What is an "untimed" test?
   b. What is a criterion-referenced test?
   c. Was the teacher properly and adequately trained to administer the test?
   d. What are your views about the size of the test group?
5. What do we know about Dee? How does our knowledge of Dee affect this case?
6. Did the teachers, administrators, and guidance counselor handle this situation properly? Why or why not?

FOR FURTHER REFLECTION

1. Do you think the teacher's actions would have been different if the test were a classroom test? Why or why not?

2. Do you think the teacher's actions would have been different if the test were a norm-referenced test? Why or why not?
3. How can a teacher maintain decorum in a testing situation when students finish at different rates?
4. What should be included in test training sessions?
5. Should students with disabilities be tested in the "mainstream"?
6. If you were the test coordinator at this school, how would this case affect your future planning?
7. How do you think this situation might have differed if students had been seventh-graders? Sixth-graders?
8. Would you describe the teacher as a behaviorist, a developmentalist, or a humanist?

FOR SCHOOL LEADERS

1. Which ISLLC standards apply to this case?
2. What should an administrator's role be in testing? Planning? Conducting/administering? Preparing students?
3. How important is student test performance to the school administrator?
4. In what ways do administrators pressure students and teachers to perform on tests? Are these actions appropriate? How can a principal monitor his or her behavior?

CHAPTER SEVEN

Day In and Day Out

"I don't get it."

"What don't you get, Steve?"

"I don't get the whole thing!" Steve's reply was greeted by groans from the entire class. It was the third time this week that Steve "didn't get it."

"You're so stupid!"

"Why don't you pay attention?"

Like some of the students, I wished Steve would pay attention when I gave the lesson and the assignment. I was writing on the side board and was not standing next to Steve's desk to help him stay focused. Several moments elapsed while I shepherded the students back to their own work and before I could get Steve to comprehend the explanations he had missed.

I was in my second year of teaching at Creekside Middle School, a middle-sized school in a bedroom community of a small southern city. Creekside students ranged from very poor to upper middle class. But in the past five years, the at-risk population in the school had tripled from 10 percent to 30 percent. Minority students, predominantly African American, constituted 20 percent of the school population.

As a nontraditional student who had gone back to college in my midthirties after my own children were ensconced in school activities, I was excited to be teaching at Creekside. My college program had emphasized the latest trends in education, and Creekside embodied the middle school concept. Our principal had fully embraced the principles of middle-level education. He was on state advisory committees and was president of the state middle school association. A few years earlier, he had pulled his faculty, kicking and screaming, into the new philosophy.

One of the most important concepts I had studied was teaming. I believed in teaming and so did Creekside. Unfortunately, my expectations for teaming and team spirit were not fulfilled during my first year of teaching. I was a floater that year—moving from classroom to classroom with my materials loaded on a cart. As I floated through classrooms, I found that not all teachers had been won over to the teaming concept.

Hence, when an odd number of teachers was required for the next year, another new teacher and I volunteered to leave our five-person teams and create a two-person team. She and I had similar expectations and wanted to try some new ideas without the confines of a large team. It also alleviated the established teams from making unwanted changes.

Having my own classroom seemed like heaven. During the summer, my new teammate and I had spent hours planning. We established team rules, created interdisciplinary units, developed advisory activities, and planned field trips. We were so excited that we didn't mind preparing for the new subject areas that came with our assignment.

On a two-person team like ours, the sixty students have only two teachers to instruct five academic subjects. I taught science, language arts, and reading to one group while my partner taught science, math, and social studies to her group. Then we switched groups and I taught language arts and reading to the new group and she taught math and social studies to my old group. The two-person team configuration provides teachers a greater opportunity to nurture their students than the five-person team where each teacher has five different groups of students. As a result, immature students, students with problems of organization, or students with other special considerations were placed on our team. Steve was one of those students.

Steve carried a lot of baggage to school. He took medication for attention deficit hyperactivity disorder and attended a resource class for assistance with written expression. Immature, with underdeveloped social skills, he had a history of being victimized by other students' bullying. His overprotective parents, particularly his mother, made excuses for him or even completed his work for him. Family counseling had been suggested during sixth grade, but had not occurred.

Students who had attended school with Steve during the previous grades did not like him. They scrutinized his every move, waiting for him to err, so they could call attention to his mistake. They valued harassing Steve more highly than they valued avoiding punishment for their misbehavior. Teasing and verbal attacks were a part of all too many classes.

Steve did not seem to understand his part in these altercations. He was eager to please me and his other teachers. He appeared pleasant and conscientious about his work. But he often instigated problems with other students by teasing them. He was just having fun, but he didn't know when to stop. The other student would get mad, and yet Steve would not quit. He didn't know how to ignore anyone's comments. In Steve's mind, the arguments were always someone else's fault.

Many students picked on Steve and were vocal in their dislike of him, but six were particularly dedicated to disturbing him. Sometimes, I thought an unseen conductor orchestrated their outbursts. Three of the sextet were girls and three were boys. The girls, Jennifer, Heather, and LaToya, were friends in class but did not pal around outside class. They were bright, capable students whose names often appeared on the honor roll. Their primary attack strategy was loud, biting comments.

The boys were similarly capable students, but they were immature and rarely applied themselves to their class work. Brian was the master at keeping the cauldron simmering. Although he sometimes made comments directly to Steve, more often he would goad another student into attacking Steve and then he would egg them on. Brian was "Mr. Personality" and everyone wanted to be his friend. So it was not difficult for him to find minions to do his Steve-work. He enjoyed stirring the pot and watching it boil over.

Brian was small, but he did not suffer over his size like David, the fifth member of the sextet. David was not popular. He had difficulty making and maintaining friendships. Occasionally the outbursts were directed at him instead of Steve.

R. J. was desperately seeking his identity. He had changed his name from Roger, had his ear pierced on the school courtyard, and sported outrageous haircuts including a shaved head. R. J.'s achievement measures fluctuated wildly. He sought Brian's friendship, hence the allegiance to the Steve attack.

During the school year, Steve and LaToya were suspended for fighting during one incident, and Steve and David were suspended after another. My teammate and I developed an elaborate scheme to keep Steve and the other students from going to their lockers at the same time. Hallway time seemed to incubate the scuffles.

Incidents with other students were only part of the problem, however. Steve was a magician at making noninstructional objects appear. He couldn't pay attention to his work because his hands and mind were occupied with marbles, tape measures, baseball cards, and countless other objects. My desk drawer was filled with Steve's possessions. His mother wrote a note asking for their return. I said I would entrust them only to a parent, and she promised that no more toys would surface at school. But they did.

To control this behavior, I seated Steve in the center of the front row of class. This seating seemed to help him stay focused. It also protected him from the other students who would plant objects in his book bag and then accuse Steve of stealing.

Seating was not the only measure I tried. The guidance counselor became our partner in developing systems to control Steve and modify his behaviors. We conferenced with Steve. We devised a reward system for him. We conferenced with the other students and responded to *every* inappropriate behavior. We assigned them detention for their verbal outbursts and harassment. We assigned them essays about their behavior. We sent the students individually to the counselor. They went as a group. And then the group and Steve met with her. The counselor and we teachers met with Steve and his mother. Temporarily and grudgingly a truce would be drawn.

But the students still did not want to work with Steve. Cooperative groups, which were an integral part of my instructional format, were stymied in Steve's groups. Even when Steve contributed his share of work and materials, students chafed at working with him. Reinforcing positive social skills through cooperative activities became a real challenge.

Cooperative Learning

Cooperative learning is a teaching method by which students are grouped. The goals of cooperative learning include learning from one's peers and student cooperation. The group work may be graded as a whole or grades may be assigned individually. Cooperative learning works best when each student in the group has a role: leader/facilitator, monitor, recorder, reporter, timekeeper.

Toward the end of the year, I could see some changes in Steve. He learned to ignore the behavior of his detractors. He could actually recognize that he had initiated some incidents himself. But often the taunts would pierce the classroom air, and I would hear:

"I don't get it."

"Aw, why don't you pay attention, Steve?!"

DISCUSSION QUESTIONS

1. What is this case about?
   a. What was the teacher's problem from her point of view?
   b. From your point of view?
2. What do we know about the teacher?
   a. What do we know about the teacher's background?
   b. What do we know about her teacher training?
   c. What do we know about her previous teaching experience?
   d. What is a "floater"?
   e. How would you characterize this teacher?
3. What do we know about the school community?
   a. How would you describe the school community?
   b. Would you describe the school as a "true" middle school? Why or why not?
   c. What are the advantages and disadvantages of two- and five-person teams?
4. What do we know about Steve?
   a. How would you characterize Steve?
   b. How would you describe Steve's background?
   c. Is Steve a typical seventh-grader?
   d. How would you explain Steve's behavior?
   e. Did Steve deserve what he got?
5. How would you characterize the other students?
   a. Describe Jennifer, Heather, LaToya, Brian, David, and R. J.
   b. How does each typify adolescence?
   c. What reasons might you suggest for the behavior of each?
6. What other interventions would you suggest for solving this dilemma?
   a. What should be the role of the guidance counselor?
   b. How could the school and home communities work together more effectively?

FOR FURTHER REFLECTION

1. Is there a way to a fresh start for Steve?
2. What impact do floating teachers have on the team concept?
3. How might cooperative groups be used to advance the social skills of middle schoolers?

FOR SCHOOL LEADERS

1. Which ISLLC standards apply to this case?
2. What are the advantages and disadvantages of two- and five-person teams?
3. Are two-person teams more nurturing? Should Steve have been placed in this team?
4. How does one decide which teachers should "float"?
5. What is the school administrator's role in this case?

CHAPTER EIGHT

A Causal Link?

I began my twelfth year of teaching resource classes excited and curious. Meeting my new sixth-grade students was always fun. It would also be wonderful to see the seventh- and eighth-grade students, some of whom would be in my classes again this year. I was always surprised to see how much some of my students, especially the boys, had changed over the summer.

The first day was going smoothly. I thoroughly enjoyed all of the classes I had had so far. "This is going to be a wonderful year," I thought as I waited for the students for my last class of the day to arrive.

Teaching in this district is challenging and energizing. Our school is generally considered to be the most desirable of the three middle schools in the district. Since the school opened eight years ago, the number of minority students has risen steadily, but the students are still predominantly white and from middle- and upper-middle-class families.

The district itself is medium-sized and growing. It is ranked among the top in the state. Families flock to the area so that their children can attend our schools. Many of the parents are actively involved in their children's education—at the *elementary* level. Just like many other districts, however, the involvement often declines when the children reach middle school.

As the eight students tumbled into the classroom during last period, I thought about what I knew of them. Seven of them were sixth-graders and one was a seventh-grader. The seventh-grader was classified as emotionally disabled. Five of the students were boys. This was not an uncommon grouping in a learning disabilities (LD) class, and all of the sixth-graders were classified as LD. LD is defined as a significant discrepancy between the student's intelligence quotient (IQ) and his achievement scores. A significant discrepancy is considered to be present if there is at least a fifteen percentile point difference between the two scores.

After the students were seated, I called the roll and took care of other housekeeping matters. Next, I went over the class rules. Then I launched into my speech about how the resource class could be a tool to help improve students' grades in their regular classes. As I scanned the room, I noticed Terrance White sprawled in his chair. He appeared bored and uninterested. He had already interrupted me several times by laughing, making inappropriate comments, and talking to the students around him. Each time he had been disruptive, I had stopped class and reminded him that one of the rules was to be respectful when someone else was speaking. My reminders appeared to have no effect, and the other students seemed to enjoy Terrance's antics. Terrance was the first person out of the door when I dismissed the class. Frankly, I was relieved when the bell rang, signaling the end of class. I sank into my chair exhausted and frustrated.

I didn't have the opportunity to read through Terrance's current Individual Education Plan (IEP) until the following afternoon. I read the current plan and his previous ones. I discovered that Terrance had been in a resource learning disabilities class in third grade, but had been in a self-contained learning disabilities class in fourth grade and part of fifth grade. In February of the previous year, Terrance had been moved from the self-contained class to a resource class. He had been scheduled for one period of resource for the remainder of the school year. The current year would be the first full year in several years in which he would be scheduled for regular academic classes for the majority of the day. Studying his reading, math, and written expression scores from the Peabody Individual Achievement Test (PIAT), I was shocked at this schedule. He had not scored above the mid-third-grade level in reading or spelling and he was weak in written expression. How could this student be expected to succeed in regular sixth-grade classes with only one period of resource assistance?

Terrance's IEP specified that he should receive one period of resource per day to assist him with reading and language arts. It is difficult to provide adequate resource assistance in two subject areas in only one class period, especially if the student is weak academically in both areas.

Concerned about being able to provide adequate services to this student, I telephoned Terrance's house and spoke with his mother. I carefully explained my reservations about Terrance receiving only one period of resource per day. I suggested that a second period be added and that I instruct him for primary reading. I would be his only reading teacher, and he would be reading material on his instructional level of second grade instead of on a sixth-grade level. He could also drop his social studies

---

Individualized Education Program

STUDENT'S NAME: Terrance White

MEDICAID NR: NA

BIRTHDATE: 04/28/82

PROJECTED SCHOOL: Emsworth Middle School

GRADE: 6

MEETING DATE: 05/25/94

EVALUATION DATE: 06/27/93

RELATED SERVICES NEEDED PER WEEK
No services needed at this time

MINUTES OR PERIODS IN REGULAR ED: 35

IN SPECIAL ED/RELATED SERVICES: 5

PHYSICAL EDUCATION: Regular

VOCATIONAL EDUCATION: N/A

CANDIDATE TYPE: N/A

STANDARDIZED TESTING

Readiness: N/A

SUB TESTS

Statewide: N/A	Read Voc:	N/A	Read Comp: N/A	Lang Exp:	N/A
	Lang Mech:	N/A	Spelling: N/A	Listening:	N/A
	Soc. Sci.:	N/A	Study Sk: N/A	Science:	N/A
	Num Concept: N/A		Math Appl: N/A	MathComp:	N/A

SAP: YES Reading: YES Math: YES Writing: YES Science: YES

ACCOMMODATIONS NEEDED: No special accommodations needed

Exit Exam: N/A   Reading: N/A   Math: N/A   Writing: N/A

PLACEMENT MODEL: Primary LD Resource
CLASSIFICATION: Learning Disabilities

INITITATION DATE OF SERVICES: 08/18/94
ANTICIPATED DURATION OF SERVICES: 06/02/95
ANTICIPATED ANNUAL REVIEW: 05/25/95
DISCIPLINE PLAN: Same as a regular student at Emsworth Middle
School

Page 2

LRE Instructional Status

NAME: Terrance White

Transition Services
__*__   N/A for this student
_____   Transition services are included in the IEP
_____   Student's interests and preferences

_____
_____
_____

Extended School Year
_____   Extended school year has been considered and is appropriate at this time
__*__   Extended school year has been considered and is not appropriate at this time

Promotion/Retention
__*__   No alternative promotion/retention standards required
_____   Alternative promotion/standards are required:

_____
_____

Supplemental Services	Extent			
_____ Itinerant	_____ /week	__*__ Resource	5 periods /week	
_____ Interpreting	_____ /week	_____ Tutoring	_____ /week	
_____ Consultation	_____ /week	_____ Notetaking	_____ /week	
_____ _____	_____ /week	_____ _____	_____ /week	

Description of specific supplementary service to be provided:
Primary written expression, basic reading, reading comprehension

Supplementary Aids (check all that apply)

_____ classroom modifications		__*__ instructional adaptations	
_____ time management		_____ augmentative communication	
_____ large print / braille texts		_____ auditory trainer / amplification	
_____ curriculum adaptation		_____ behavior management (plan attached)	
_____ assistive technology device(s)		_____ _____	
_____ _____		_____ _____	

Description of specific supplementary aids to be provided:
Terrance should be able to have Social Studies and Science tests read to him. His spelling should not be penalized except on spelling test. Teacher provides notes for Social Studies and Science. Allowed to use Word Master in regular class setting.
LRE Recommendations:

Is this student to be removed from the regular educational environment?
_____ yes   _____ no   (if yes, complete LRE 1,11)

Is this student to be placed in the school he or she would normally attend if not disabled?
_____ yes   _____ no   (if no, complete LRE 1,11)

Page 3

Individualized Education Program

NAME: Terrance White

_____ I have attended the IEP/LRE meeting, I understand the IEP/LRE process and have participated as an equal member of the committee in developing this IEP and in determining the least restrictive environment and placement for my child. I have read the IEP/LRE documents or had them read to me, understand their contents and agree with the educational and related services to be provided to my child as delineated in this IEP/LRE. I understand I will receive a copy of the IEP/LRE documents.

_____ I did not attend the IEP meeting, but was given the opportunity to do so. I understand and agree with the contents of the IEP/LRE. I have received a copy of the IEP/LRE.

_____   ___/___/___
(parent/ surrogate parent/ legal guardian)   (date)

COMMITTEE MEMBERS:

I have participated as an equal member of the IEP committee in the review and development of this IEP and its Least Restrictive Environment (LRE) components for this pupil. I verify that all LRE components were discussed and considered during the IEP meeting, and that the pupil's placement is based on the completed IEP and the LRE requirements of P.L. 94-142 (as amended). My signature below indicates agreement with the educational and related services to be provided to this student as delineated in this document.

COMMITTEE SIGNATURES

Name	Position	Date
_____	Parent/Legal Guardian	___/___/___
_____	Special Ed Instructor	___/___/___
_____	L.E.A.	___/___/___
_____	_____	___/___/___
_____	_____	___/___/___
_____	_____	___/___/___
_____	_____	___/___/___
_____	_____	___/___/___
_____	_____	___/___/___
_____	_____	___/___/___

Chapter 8

Page 4

Individualized Education Program
Present Levels of Performance

NAME: Terrance White

ACHIEVEMENT TESTS:

DATE: 0/4/26/94   TEST: PIAT-R
SCORES:

gen. information:	6.8 grade equiv.	reading recog.:	2.0 grade equiv.
reading comp.:	2.9 grade equiv.	total reading:	2.4 grade equiv.
math:	5.9 grade equiv.	spelling:	3.2 grade equiv.
written language:	80 standard		

STUDENT'S READING ABILITY: Terrance uses basic decoding skills (CVC, CVVC, CVCE). He can tell you the main idea of a short story.

STUDENT'S MATH ABILITY: Terrance can add, subtract, multiply, and divide double digit numbers.

LEARNING CONSIDERATIONS:

STRENGTHS: Terrance is well liked by his peers. He gives 100 percent when he is interested in an activity. He has a lot of common sense. He can add, subtract, and multiply fractions.

WEAKNESSES: Terrance has difficulty decoding and spelling words with irregular consonant and vowel sound. He has problems writing the summary of a story in a paragraph.

SPECIFIC DISABILITIES: Written Expression; Basic Reading; Reading Comprehension

Individualized Education Program
Present Levels of Performance

NAME: Terrance White

ACHIEVEMENT TESTS:

DATE: 04/06/95   TEST: Woodcock-Johnson

SCORES:
reading: 2.7 grade equiv.   mathematics: 5.2 grade equiv.
written language: 2.4 grade equiv.   knowledge: 5.0 grade equiv.
skills: 3.3 grade equiv.

STUDENT'S READING ABILITY: cannot keep up in the content subjects due to low reading ability

STUDENT'S MATH ABILITY: does not qualify as a disabled student but is not doing well in subject area

LEARNING CONSIDERATIONS:
STRENGTHS: volunteers in class

WEAKNESSES: poor phonetic skills makes decoding words difficult, poor language skills hinder writing skills, poor comprehension skills

SPECIFIC DISABLITIES: Written Expression; Basic Reading; Reading Comprehension

Student Name:	White, Terrance	
Student Number:	010046012	Sex: M
Birth Date:	4/28/82	

CLASS SCHEDULE

Per	Days	Subject	Teacher	Room
First	Semester			
1	MTWRF	Home Base	Simms	805
2	MTWRF	Jostens 6th Grade	Glenn	812
3	MTWRF	Language Arts	Ray	806
4	MTWRF	Reading	Ray	806
5	MTWRF	Social Studies	Ray	806
6	MTWRF	Lunch	Simms	805
7	MTWRF	Science	Simms	805
8	MTWRF	Resource Reading/Writing Exp.	North	301
9	MTWRF	Math	Simms	805

class because it was not a state-tested subject. I made this latter suggestion thinking that one fewer academic subject would be advisable for
Terrance. Terrance's mother was nice enough, but she was unable to
come to school for a conference. She refused permission for a second period of resource to be added to Terrance's schedule.

Terrance was on a two-person team. In addition to the resource assistance in reading and language arts, he was scheduled for the computer lab
for additional help in mathematics. Over the next few weeks, the number
of behavior problems on the team increased steadily. This was particularly true in the following classes: reading, language arts, social studies,
and computer lab. All of these classes were taught by young white fe-
males. He was openly hostile toward the computer lab teacher and usually refused to do his assignments. In reading and language arts, he completed some of his class assignments, but he turned in little homework.
Terrance frequently interrupted the classes by talking out and laughing at
inappropriate times.

The team felt that it was important to try to bring his behavior under
control quickly. His parents were telephoned and a conference was
scheduled. This time, Mrs. White attended the conference. Things went

smoothly. The regular class teachers, the guidance counselor, and I all presented our concerns. We decided to give Terrance additional class-room modifications including taking regular class tests in the resource class as needed, having me read aloud tests or sections of tests as needed, introducing the first ten words for a twenty-word spelling unit on Monday and taking the test on those words on Wednesday, and introducing the second ten words from the unit on Wednesday and testing these words on Friday.

Mrs. White agreed with our recommendations and said that Terrance would be disciplined at home whenever he was disruptive at school. To make sure he completed his homework assignments, Terrance was to record his assignments daily in an assignment book. Mrs. White pledged to check the notebook daily. She said, "I want my son to get a good education. My husband and I agree that a good education is important."

As the conference concluded, Mrs. White gave us her husband's phone number at work. "Please call my husband when Terrance misbehaves or doesn't do his work." I felt more hopeful as I left the meeting.

My hopefulness was short-lived. Within a few days, Terrance was again wreaking havoc both inside and outside the classroom. By Christmas break, his behavior had deteriorated even further. Most of the sixth-graders were intimidated by his height. He was the tallest student in my classes by a good three inches. He wasn't heavy, but he was solidly built and strong. He began to demand items from other students: textbooks, pencils, pens, paper, and even money. They usually complied. In my class, I controlled the situation as best I could. Punishment for his inappropriate behavior included writing assignments, lunch detention, suspension from school. Parent contact was made or attempted every time Terrance was given any punishment other than a writing assignment. Calls to his father were being made once a week or more.

After Christmas, the situation did not improve. Parent contact was maintained, but it no longer seemed effective. His father listened, "Hmmed," and seemed totally disinterested. Calls to his mother garnered the same response.

Behavior problems continued to increase. Toward the end of February, Terrance threatened to return to computer lab with a "lethal weapon." He was referred to the district's director of special services for a conference, after which he was permitted to return to school.

Things came to a head in mid-April when he hit a student in the chest with so much force that the other student was confined to the nurse's station for two hours. The sixth-grade administrator suspended Terrance from school for three days and referred him a second time to the director of special services. The parents were requested to attend a conference to discuss the situation.

Mrs. White attended the meeting as did the sixth-grade administrator, the school psychologist, the sixth-grade guidance counselor, Terrance's two regular teachers, the computer lab teacher, and myself. We all sat stiffly around a large oval conference table. I think we all silently wondered what the outcome of the meeting would be. It was the first meeting that I had ever attended where the causal link factor was an issue.

The sixth-grade administrator spoke first. He opened a manila folder. In a firm voice, he briefly and clearly explained each of the twenty-one behavior infractions. Next, he explained that the purpose of the meeting was to determine if there was a causal link between Terrance's handicapping condition and his behavior.

The school psychologist defined the term "causal link." "Causal link means a direct link is present between a handicapping condition and the behaviors exhibited by the student. In other words, is the student's handicapping condition *causing* him to behave inappropriately? This is the question the group must answer," she said.

I explained the nature of Terrance's disability and reviewed his test scores from the Wide Range Achievement Test-Revised (WRAT-R) that I had administered in March. Terrance had scored low in all areas except math and science. "He has a great deal of difficulty academically. It is no wonder Terrance is not able to do most of the sixth-grade work required of him in his regular classes. I recommend that the group meet again to discuss whether placement in a Learning Disabilities Self Contained (LDSC) classroom might be a more appropriate placement for next year."

I explained that a LDSC class is much smaller than a regular class. "There are presently two full-time teacher assistants in the class. The same material is covered but at a slower pace than in the regular class. Material is often presented orally as well as in writing."

I concluded by saying, "Terrance is weak in a number of areas. He needs to go back and learn basic information he should have learned in the lower grades. If he does not learn the basics, he will continue to fall further and further behind his peers." I wondered how Mrs. White would react to what I said, but she made no comment.

Terrance's regular teachers described his behavioral and academic problems in turn. Finally, the guidance counselor spoke about her interactions with Terrance throughout the year.

The school psychologist called for us to answer the causal link question. She began with a "No," indicating she felt there was no causal link between his disability and his inappropriate behavior. One by one, the committee members responded in kind, without hesitation. Mrs. White was the last respondent. "Yes," she stated.

I clarified, "Do you feel Terrance's inappropriate behavior is caused by a learning disability in reading and written expression?"

"Yes, I think it could be," she responded.

"Please explain why you feel that way," I asked.

"Terrance can't read very well, and he gets upset," she replied.

Frustrated, I continued, "I have read tests aloud to Terrance and he does not usually appear to be paying attention. I have read selections aloud to him and I have had other students read aloud to him. He does not pay attention. I have given extra days to study for tests and he tells me later than he did not study. Assignments have been broken down or shortened so he will not feel overwhelmed. The assignments are still not completed. We have made every reasonable accommodation to help him. His progress has declined all year. He is failing every class except math. Since you feel there is a causal link between his handicapping condition and his behavior problems, how do you feel about putting Terrance in an LDSC class next year?"

"I do not want to put him in that class," she responded.

"You are telling us there is a causal link, but you do not want to put him in the type of class where he would receive the most help. I do not understand." I could hear the frustration in my own voice.

The school psychologist explained that the committee must be in total agreement before the paper could be signed. We would have to meet again to try to reach agreement.

The sixth-grade administrator stated that Terrance could not return to school due to the severity of several of the discipline infractions. Terrance would be able to receive homebound instruction if the causal link paper were signed, showing unanimous agreement that Terrance's behavior was not linked to his disability. The meeting was adjourned without the issue being resolved.

DISCUSSION QUESTIONS

1. What is this case about?
   a. What was the teacher's problem from her point of view? From your point of view?
   b. What should the teacher do next?

2. What do we know about Terrance?
   a. How would you describe Terrance?
   b. What is his grade level? What kinds of problems might this introduce?
   c. How does Terrance mesh with the school and student characteristics?
   d. What kind of behavior problems did Terrance exhibit?
   e. What could have been some of the reasons for Terrance's behavior?
   f. Did his disability contribute to his behavior? Explain your answer.
   g. What was Terrance's relationship with his teachers?
3. What do we know about the teacher?
   a. How would you describe the teacher?
   b. What role does the teacher's experience play in this case?
   c. Does the teacher exhibit any biases?
   d. What instructional techniques did the teacher use to try to solve the problem?
   e. What other techniques might have worked?
   f. Were the teacher's expectations reasonable?
4. What do we know about the school community?
   a. How would you describe the school community?
   b. How does the school community relate to the case?
5. Did the teacher gather adequate information to solve the problem prior to calling the parent the first time?
   a. What kind of information did the teacher gather?
   b. What is an IEP? What information did it provide?
6. How does this case relate to the issue of parent involvement?
   a. Do you agree with the teacher's conclusion that parent involvement lessens in the middle school? How can more parent involvement be encouraged, or should it be?
   b. Were Terrance's parents involved with his education?
   c. If you were Terrance's parent, how would you react to the initial call made by the teacher? The causal link conference?
7. Do race and gender play a role in this case? What race and gender were the teacher?
8. What is the role of the resource class in a student's education?
   a. Were the services the teacher provided beneficial?
   b. What do you think of the teacher's suggestion to add another period of resource in lieu of social studies?
   c. Should Terrance be placed in a self-contained classroom?

9. A number of references are made to physical development in this case. What role does it play in this case? In the middle school?
10. Did the teacher solve the problem by scheduling a conference?
    a. Was a conference an appropriate approach to solving the problem?
    b. Were the appropriate participants invited?
    c. Should Terrance have been included?
    d. What was the outcome of the conference?
11. Was there any warning that Terrance would have harmed another student?
    a. Could the incident have been avoided? How?
    b. Do you think that there was a causal link?

FOR FURTHER REFLECTION

1. What will become of Terrance's future?
2. Does the school have a responsibility to follow up on the causal link meeting?

FOR SCHOOL LEADERS

1. Which ISLLC standards apply to this case?
2. What is the school administrator's role in this case?

CHAPTER NINE

Patrice

At Cedar Grove Middle School a high level of enthusiasm could be felt throughout the building. It was the first week of school and it was the first year of implementation of the middle school concept. It was also the first week of middle school for the sixth-graders—new school, new teachers, changing classes—all things to anticipate.

I had an ideal teaching situation. I was scheduled to teach four social studies classes and one reading class. My teaching team consisted of highly motivated, true professionals. We had spent the summer rearranging classrooms and planning interdisciplinary units and advisory activities. Anyone could have mistaken us for sixth-graders in our excitement over our team logo and our team costumes. We anticipated the first day of school no less than the incoming sixth-graders.

Advisory Program

Advisory programs are formalized programs that enable students to meet with teachers and other students to discuss personal concerns. Premised on the notion that each student will formulate an "advisory" relationship with at least one teacher, most programs consist of regularly scheduled classes with set meeting times. The most common schedules are once a day or once a week. Some advisory programs have set curricula such as decision-making programs or study skills or values clarification.

First-day thrill over the middle school concept appeared to carry over the next several weeks for the students. They were well behaved and wanted to participate in the activities we had planned. But a change soon came over one student named Patrice.

How well I recall my first incident with Patrice! I was checking home-work and everyone had their assignments—until I came to Patrice. Patrice had always completed her assignments prior to this day, so I was a little surprised to find none of her homework done.

"Don't have it," she muttered when I stopped beside her desk.

"Why don't you have your homework, Patrice?" I asked quietly.

Patrice shrugged her shoulders and rolled her eyes. "No remorse," I thought. Patrice's behavior toward me was disrespectful, but I maintained my composure and decided to address the matter after class.

I began my lesson and noticed that Patrice was not paying attention. She didn't have her book out as I had requested, so I paused and asked her to "please take out your book." She complied, but not without slamming her book on the desk, rolling her eyes, and sucking her teeth. I had to re-spond; the entire class was watching me. "If you do not care to learn, you are welcome to sit outside while we have class."

Patrice left. I panicked! I was shocked; it wasn't the reaction I expected. I continued with class thinking that I would let Patrice sit outside and stew for a bit. Once the class was busy with the assignment, I stepped outside to confer with Patrice who seemed to be enjoying her time out.

"I can't understand why you were so rude to me in the classroom. You know it's your responsibility to complete your homework and participate in class."

Patrice sucked her teeth.

"Do you realize that you disrupted the entire class?" I asked.

Patrice shrugged her shoulders.

"Would you like to come back and join the class?" I inquired.

She shrugged her shoulders again, a sign that she didn't care. But I did; I knew she couldn't spend the remainder of the class outside. So, I told Patrice to return to the classroom and get started on the assignment like everyone else. Patrice went to her desk and opened her book, but she did not start working on the assignment. She watched the clock. I moved to-ward her desk and showed her the page for the assignment, stating, "Get busy." Patrice smirked but appeared to start on the assignment. When I collected papers at the end of class, her paper said "Patrice" and nothing more. Rather than question her further that day, I decided to discuss this in a team meeting.

During the team meeting, I described what had happened with Patrice during fourth period. My teammates had noticed some of the same be-haviors that I had experienced. She had completed few of the assignments in English and math. We reviewed what we knew about Patrice. She was

African American, living in a single-parent home. There was no evidence whatsoever of her father. Her sister was enrolled in special education classes in another school. We decided to call her mother, Mrs. Johnson, and request a conference.

Mrs. Johnson was pleasant and supportive on the telephone. She told me that Patrice was excited about school and talked about her assignments at home. She agreed to meet with the team.

The conference went smoothly. We took turns informing Mrs. Johnson about Patrice's incomplete assignments and rude and disruptive behaviors. After our remarks, we solicited Mrs. Johnson's input. She scanned our faces and said, "You all look fine to me. You have nice faces. You really need to be tough with Patrice."

Patrice's behaviors did not change, but we tolerated them for the first quarter, hoping they might change with our "toughness." During the second quarter, we enlisted the help of the guidance counselor, Mrs. Stone. The team met with Mrs. Stone as a group, and then Mrs. Stone met with Patrice and put her on a behavior contract. The contract listed three items for improvement:

- coming to class on time,
- completing homework and classwork,
- not sucking teeth.

The contract was to be signed daily by all teachers at the conclusion of class. After just one afternoon, Patrice had misplaced her contract sheet and decided that she did not want to continue with "this stupid contract."

Patrice's inappropriate behaviors escalated over the next few weeks. She used obscene language and then threatened students who reported her behavior. She began making phone calls to teachers. Sometimes she would call and hang up as soon as someone answered, but at other times she would yell obscenities. We suspected Patrice's handiwork in these calls, and our suspicions were confirmed with phone traces. I changed my phone number and to this day have an unlisted number.

Her behavior was intolerable, and in a meeting with the teachers, guidance counselor, and assistant principal, Patrice was informed of the consequences for her continued misbehavior: in-school suspension, out-of-school suspension, and possible expulsion. To cover all bases, Patrice was tested for special education placement (for which she did not qualify).

In-School Suspension

In-school suspension programs remove from the classroom students who have been discipline problems. Students are relocated within the school and monitored. Teachers assign work that is to be completed during the in-school suspension period. In-school suspension is advantageous over out-of-school suspension in that it enables students to remain in school and complete their classwork. It does not carry as pejorative a connotation as out-of-school suspension, which is often the next level of punishment.

During the third quarter, Patrice spent an inordinate amount of time in in-school suspension. She was suspended (out-of-school) for days at a time. I must admit those were some of the most enjoyable days of the school year for me.

In March, the assistant principal chased out to my car after school to tell me the good news: Patrice would appear before the constituent school board for an expulsion hearing. However, there was one hitch. We had to try one last intervention: shared responsibility. Shared responsibility is a program that involves parents. Mrs. Johnson would be required to spend a day with Patrice in school. She would attend all classes and activities. The philosophy behind the program was to exhibit the inappropriate behavior to parents so they would be aware of the reasons for disciplinary action.

Patrice did not modify her behavior in her mother's presence, but her mother slept through most of the school day. During the daily team meeting, which both Patrice and her mother attended, Mrs. Johnson offered but one solution. She exclaimed, "Patrice does not have a chance at this school. I want her transferred to another school."

The school board hearing resulted in suspension for Patrice. She failed the school year and returned to Cedar Grove as a sixth-grader again the following year. She was placed with another team where she sat quietly in the back of the room in each class. She didn't complete her assignments and she didn't participate in class. She didn't pass sixth grade that year either, but due to her previous retention was placed into the seventh grade.

DISCUSSION QUESTIONS

1. What is this case about?
2. What do we know about the teacher?
3. What do we know about the school?
   a. What were the teachers' attitudes about the middle school concept?
   b. What were the students' attitudes about the middle school concept?
4. What do we know about Patrice and Mrs. Johnson?
   a. How would you characterize Patrice as a student? How did her behavior change over the course of the case?
   b. Describe Mrs. Johnson. How did her behavior change over the course of the case?
5. Discuss some alternate ways of handling Patrice's behavior in class.
   a. Was Patrice's behavior "disrespectful"?
   b. The teacher said, "I had to respond. The entire class was watching me." What is your opinion of this statement?
   c. What is your view of the teacher's statement "If you do not care to learn, you are welcome to sit outside while we have class"?
   d. Should a teacher send a student outside the classroom?
6. The teachers were excited about the middle school concept. Were they actually able to make a transition to the true concept? Support your answer with excerpts from the case.
7. What role do race, gender, and culture play in this case?
   a. In the teacher's actions/viewpoints?
   b. In Patrice's actions?
   c. In Mrs. Johnson's actions?
8. Was there any value in the behavior contract?
   a. Were the correct actions targeted?
   b. Should the teachers and counselor have abandoned the contract so easily?
9. What are your views of shared responsibility?
10. Do you think that Mrs. Johnson was right in requesting that Patrice be transferred to another school?
11. What action could be taken to "save" Patrice? Is there a second chance for her?

FOR FURTHER REFLECTION

1. Should the teacher take legal action against Patrice for the phone calls?
2. Are there some students that we, as teachers, cannot reach? Should these students be ignored? To what extent is the teacher responsible for Patrice's future?

FOR SCHOOL LEADERS

1. Which ISLLC standards apply to this case?
2. Would you recommend suspension or expulsion in this case?
3. What other recommendations would you have made to the teachers and board?
4. What responsibility does an administrator have for protecting teachers from students?

CHAPTER TEN

Starting in the Middle

My first year as a professional teacher wasn't actually a year long. I began my tenure at Evergreen Middle School in the middle of the year—at the start of the second semester when my predecessor, Mrs. Miller, resigned. I will never forget my thoughts and feelings as I entered Room 605 for the first time.

I was confident of myself and my abilities, having received a first-rate education and intensive teacher training at a highly reputed university. I had taken courses in the latest educational methods and theories as well as a course on multiculturalism. We had read and discussed cases. I had observed for hundreds of hours in classrooms, and for an entire semester I had tutored at-risk students at a nearby middle school. All of this preparation culminated with an exciting and meaningful experience during student teaching.

I was at my best as a student teacher. An unfortunate accident by my mentor teacher put me in the position of assuming all of her duties from the beginning of my teaching internship until the end. In this respect, my internship was highly unusual for aspiring educators.

The internship was set in a rural farm school with a homogeneous student body, mostly white and mostly lower middle class. The demographics of my classes and the strict discipline enforced by parents and administrators alike made my student teaching "a piece of cake." In addition, I was praised by my supervising teacher and the faculty and staff. My professors gave me high marks, culminating with the ultimate compliment from my supervisor: I was one of the best students ever to matriculate through the College of Education at the university. But an even more coveted tribute came from a student who wrote a letter extolling my virtues as a teacher to the president of the university.

Cloaked in these experiences, I was ready for the challenge of being a "real" teacher, even with a mid-year entry. As I stepped through the door-

way of Room 605, I was greeted by an energetic and personable woman—
Mrs. Miller. Mrs. Miller was a popular teacher. She commanded respect;
she was in complete control of her classes. Mrs. Miller had excellent rapport with students. She laughed and joked with them; she *knew* them all
as individuals. Furthermore, she had a "world" of knowledge about geog-
raphy, the subject of the class. It took no time for me to discern that the
students would miss her terribly. Amid the going away celebrations in
Mrs. Miller's honor, none of the students noticed her replacement. All
were focused on saying goodbye to "the best teacher in the world."

My reverie was interrupted by Mrs. Miller as she introduced me to a
shy-appearing student by the name of Amos. I had noticed Amos; he had
just given Mrs. Miller a tremendous hug. "Amos," she said, "say hello to
Mr. Boehm. He will be your new social studies and homebase (advisory
class) teacher." She turned to me, "You'll love Amos, Mr. Boehm. He's
one of our most loveable students!" Amos replied with a cheery "Hello"
and for the moment I liked him very much.

When Amos walked away, however, Mrs. Miller lowered her voice and
shared her concern about his ability to handle the upcoming change.
"Amos is a special student. He comes from a single-parent home, where
he lives with his father, who is diabetic. Amos is emotionally disturbed,
and his greatest difficulty is adjusting to change." Mrs. Miller described
how she had developed her relationship with Amos. "We weren't always
this close. One time he sat in the hallway because he refused to come to
class. Now, sometimes I have to drag him—literally, to the bus in the af-
ternoons because he's just not willing to leave class at the end of the day."

"Be careful with him, Walt," she said to me. "He's tough for everyone
to handle, but my main concern is that I am the only teacher who has
managed to connect with Amos at all this year. He might blame you once
I'm gone."

I was oblivious to Mrs. Miller's admonitions. Amos appeared so harm-
less in this first encounter. Besides, my methods courses had trained me
to deal with the needs of special students.

My first tingle of apprehension occurred a few days later. I had not yet
taken over from Mrs. Miller but was visiting the school. Mr. Powers, the
principal, approached me in the hallway. He gave me a hearty pat on the
back and inquired, "Are you ready for this new experience, Mr. Boehm?"

"I sure hope I am," I jovially replied.

After a brief chat, he asked me if I had met Amos yet. I began to feel a
little uneasy about this student. Why was the principal singling out this individual? "Amos has difficulty adjusting to different environments," Mr.

Powers stated. "Mrs. Miller and the team have worked wonders with him this year. He's grown particularly attached to Mrs. Miller. She's his buddy! He will probably resist your authority at first; you're replacing his favorite teacher. But, he'll come around. Don't worry. Based on your professors' recommendations and your training, I'm sure you'll be able to handle Amos."

Mr. Powers's words weren't the last I heard about Amos. My team leader shared some memorable stories with me and concluded: "When Amos decides to resist change, there is no moving him. He will block you. He will plant his body in his desk and refuse to cooperate. Accept it when he does; it's happened to us all."

The special education teacher agreed. "I am here to support you, Mr. Boehm. If Amos becomes a problem, I will help you in any way that I can." I would soon take advantage of this offer.

On my first day of classes, the first three class periods were positive. I explained my expectations and the incentives to the seventh-grade social studies classes. Even though the suburban Evergreen had a more diverse student body than my previous school, students seemed to respond well when I explained that other than the change of teacher, class procedures would remain the same. My words, designed to ease the transition for students, were not something Amos wanted to hear. Amos did not show up for his fourth-period social studies class that day.

Once the fourth-period students were engrossed in their assignments, I buzzed the office. Amos had been present for homebase earlier in the day; I suspected he was somewhere in the school. And he was. Amos was in the principal's office. He had informed Mr. Powers that he was not going to social studies. Mr. Powers escorted Amos back to class against his wishes. When they reached the doorway, I confronted Amos in a firm but understanding way: "Amos, why do you not want to come to social studies today?"

He responded sharply, "Because, I don't want to. I don't like you."

My confidence evaporated. Four years of preparation and ego enhancement suddenly became irrelevant. I did not know how to handle this response. I wanted Amos to like and respect me as a teacher, just like he had Mrs. Miller.

Mr. Powers propelled Amos into the classroom. I informed him of his assigned seat.

"I don't want to sit there. I don't like her!"

"Where do you want to sit, Amos?"

"I don't know."

I didn't know how to handle this response. The seating incident ruined fourth period on my first day. Once he was seated, I handed Amos a list of classroom expectations and incentives. He crumpled the sheet and threw it onto the floor. Politely, I asked Amos to pick up the paper. He said, "No. I don't want to."

I became angry and told Amos that I was the teacher now. "I am here to help you learn. I will treat you no differently than the other students." I conceded, "Maybe you and I can even write to Mrs. Miller sometime."

Amos lowered his head and folded his arms in disgust. "Where is Mrs. Miller? I hate you!" The outburst disturbed the class. But it disturbed me even more. All of the attention was focused on me and Amos. I was already faced with a confusing dilemma on my first day as a "real" teacher. How could I earn the respect and admiration of this student? How could I control outbursts like the one he had in class today? What would the rest of the students think about me if I could not get a grip on this situation?

DISCUSSION QUESTIONS

1. What is this case about?
   a. What was the teacher's problem from his point of view?
   b. From your point of view?
2. What do we know about the teacher?
   a. What do we know about the teacher's training and teaching experience?
   b. What can you discern about the teacher's personality traits?
3. What do we know about Amos? How does our knowledge of Amos affect this case?
4. What effect did starting in the middle of the year have on this case?
5. How did the information provided by Mrs. Miller, Mr. Powers, the team leader, and the special education teacher influence Mr. Boehm's actions?
   a. Was the information helpful? Harmful?
   b. Could the others have said or done anything additional to help Mr. Boehm before he met Amos?
   c. How can the others assist Mr. Boehm now?
6. What are some alternate ways for handling the first day? Should Mr. Boehm have planned something different for Amos's class knowing what he did about the student?

7. Was a "firm but understanding" approach the best one for Mr. Boehm to use with Amos? Why or why not?
   a. What is your view of Mr. Boehm's question: "Amos, why do you not want to come to social studies today?" What else might Mr. Boehm have said? What results do you think that might have produced?
   b. What is your view of Mr. Boehm's question: "Where do you want to sit, Amos?" What else might Mr. Boehm have said? What results do you think that might have produced?
   c. What is your view of Mr. Boehm's concession "Maybe you and I can even write to Mrs. Miller sometime?" What else might Mr. Boehm have said? What results do you think that might have produced?
8. What should Mr. Boehm do next?

FOR FURTHER REFLECTION

1. How would you classify Mr. Boehm in terms of his stage of adult or teacher development?
2. How should school systems deal with students like Amos?
3. How can the middle school concept affect a situation like the one presented in this case?
4. What are the pros and cons of students becoming attached to teachers?

FOR SCHOOL LEADERS

1. Which ISLLC standards apply to this case?
2. Were Mr. Powers's actions adequate for preparing Mr. Boehm to deal with Amos?
3. What are considerations for hiring new teachers in the middle of the year? Should they receive the same orientation as new hires at the beginning of the year?

CHAPTER ELEVEN

The Apathetic Student

Gerry Gacey was a new principal. He had come to Live Oak Junior High School from a larger community. Live Oak was a small town with a business section three blocks long and three blocks wide. The school was three blocks from downtown and one block from the elementary school.

Being in a small town was not the biggest adjustment though. Being in a school with seventh- and eighth-graders was the thing that was most different. Gerry had been a high school vocational teacher. He worked with students who might not have been the academic stars but they were motivated. In fact, many of his students had gone on to careers that were more lucrative than his own teaching career.

Although still in his twenties, Gerry had already moved through the ranks of teacher and assistant principal at a high school. This was the first school of his own. Things were going reasonably well, but he still couldn't get used to the student apathy. He knew that it was partly a function of age and that it was not unique to Live Oak Junior High, but he still had difficulty grasping the students' lack of understanding of the importance of an education.

Gerry could articulate the middle school position: "We find that there are so many other things that are on their list of priorities that education does not really fall into that category — it's not even in the top five. They are leaving behind the elementary mind-set of the opposite sex being ugly; they are discovering the attractiveness of the opposite sex. Their parents are giving them more responsibility. They are allowed to do things that formerly they were not allowed to do. They might be able to date or stay out later. They are starting to feel adultlike. They don't realize that they have so much further to go than Live Oak Junior High School." The challenge of dealing with middle-level learners was adding new meaning to the words themselves.

Live Oak was debating an incentive system. Gerry thought that the students were not motivated by intrinsic rewards, but by quid pro quo. Preaching was not going to work; the administrative team had decided, "we are just going to have to get down to their level."

Gerry was thinking about all of these things because of Johnson, the student he had called to the office. Johnson was a total athlete. Johnson was an excellent football player, an excellent basketball player, and an excellent baseball player. Unfortunately, it appeared that Johnson loved to come to school late. Johnson often arrived at school late, accompanied by his guardian. He seemed to just pop into school when he wanted to.

Gerry's policy required all tardy students to come to the office. Johnson rambled into the office and slouched into the chair. Gerry looked at him and said, "You know that you have been called to the office because of tardiness. Why are you late?"

"I overslept."

"You can get an alarm clock for a few dollars at Wal-Mart . . ." Before Gerry could complete his suggestion, Johnson laughed.

Gerry tried a different tack. He recounted Johnson's successes on the football field and concluded by saying that he was wasting his ability if he didn't come to school and get as much out of it as he could. "You can't get anything out of school if you aren't here. Why are you in school, Johnson?"

Johnson just looked at him. When Gerry repeated his question, Johnson appeared sheepish. Gerry rephrased the question, but the student merely mumbled a few words and grew silent. Gerry said directly, "Are you just here for the hot breakfast and the hot lunch?" Johnson smiled and appeared relieved at the joke.

Gerry set the record straight. "I'm not joking about this. There are a lot of former football players that are driving cabs and working in factories now. You have a lot of talent on the football field, but so did many of them. You know, just because you make it to the Big Show doesn't mean you're going to stay there. Only an education will guarantee you a living."

After Johnson left, Gerry thought about the conversation. The natural response to his question about attending school was "to get an education." What kind of kid couldn't even say that?

Gerry knew that Johnson had an older brother because he was a football standout at the high school. After school he headed toward the high school and watched practice wrap up. As Dwayne, Johnson's older brother, moved off the field, Gerry stopped him and asked if he could chat for a moment. Gerry explained the situation and asked, "Why does Johnson seem so out of tune with school?" Dwayne replied, "Well, we've been trying to talk with him, but he just doesn't seem to understand."

Gerry prodded gently, and Dwayne revealed that their mother had died a couple of years earlier. Dwayne said simply, "Well, Mr. Gacey, you know that's something you never get over, but I'm learning to deal with it. I think Johnson is dealing with it in his own way. And this is the way he's dealing with it."

DISCUSSION QUESTIONS

1. What is this case about?
   a. What was the principal's problem from his point of view? From your point of view?
   b. What should the principal do next?
2. What do we know about Mr. Gacey?
   a. How would you describe Gerry?
   b. What was Mr. Gacey's professional background? What role does that play in this case?
   c. How would you characterize Gerry's attitude toward middle school and middle schoolers?
3. What do we know about Johnson?
   a. How would you describe Johnson?
   b. In what ways does Johnson typify middle-level learner characteristics?
   c. Was Johnson apathetic?
4. What is your opinion of Gerry's policy of having all tardy students report to the office?
5. What is your view of Mr. Gacey's comment "You can get an alarm clock at Wal-Mart . . .?"
6. What is your view of Mr. Gacey's approach when he asked, "Why are you in school, Johnson?"
7. What is your view of Mr. Gacey's comment "Are you just here for the hot breakfast and lunch?"
8. What alternative strategies could be employed to get Johnson to school on time?
9. Do you consider Johnson to be a problem student?
10. Was it appropriate for Mr. Gacey to approach Dwayne?
11. Should the information he gained through that conversation change his approach to Johnson?

12. Did your assessment of Johnson change over the course of the case? Explain. How does this change reflect your own attitudes?
13. Did your assessment of Gerry change over the course of the case? Explain. How does this change reflect your own attitudes?

FOR FURTHER REFLECTION

1. How does this case relate to the middle school concept and precepts? How could implementation of the middle school concept impact this case?
2. What do you think about Gerry's views on an incentive system for middle-level learners? How would you design an incentive system?
3. Based on your reactions to Gerry and Johnson at the beginning of the case, would you describe yourself as a behaviorist, a developmentalist, a humanist?

FOR SCHOOL LEADERS

1. Which ISLLC standards apply to this case?
2. How could administrators be better prepared when moving from one school level to another?
3. Should middle-level principal certification be a requirement?

CHAPTER TWELVE

Culture Shock

I have traveled widely around the world, but the greatest culture shock I ever experienced was in my first year of teaching middle school. I was newly married and had moved to North Carolina to be with my Marine Corps spouse. When I stumbled onto Murraytown Middle School about twenty minutes into the country, I felt lucky to have found such a progressive school in such an unlikely spot.

Mr. Richards interviewed me and hired me on the spot. We saw eye-to-eye. He was proud of the nongraded environment at Murraytown. Students were placed into language arts classes based on their ability levels, not their ages. I was certified as a social studies teacher—secondary trained. He assigned me a social studies and language arts block. I felt prepared, having had a journalism background in high school and college.

Murraytown did not even appear to have a town attached to it. Small tobacco farms dotted the roadway. There were no shops along the way. I had grown up in a small Florida town, but it was nothing like this. The only communal aspect to the town was the school.

On the first day of school, parents—primarily mothers—accompanied their children into the classroom. They were used to new teachers since the Marine Corps created many teaching turnovers, but they wanted to introduce themselves. The first mother said to me, "This is Toy. Now you just paddle him if he gets out of line. Don't let him get by with anything." Few of the children were associated with the Marine Corps. Most of them were from farming families. The majority were white with the remainder being African American.

As the children settled in and I called the roll, my culture shock deepened. In my language arts class (classified as early sixth-grade reading level), I had fifth-grade twins named Orangejello and Lemonjello. They were the youngest and smallest children in the room, which was packed with too many students. Liora was taller than I, an eighth-grader with long flowing dirty blond-colored hair. She appeared outgoing and friendly. Todd, a tall, handsome young black man, was quiet. He was captain of the football team and seemed confident even though he spoke rarely, and when he did he was very soft-spoken. Todd's father lived in New York and Todd had spent some time there. He was one of the few students who spoke without a southern accent. Brent was a cute sixth-grader. He was slightly overage for that grade level and had recently moved to the area from Florida. I came to recognize that he was a slow learner. During the first days of school he was disoriented by his new surroundings. The faces in the class assumed names as I called the roll.

The last name on the roll produced my biggest culture shock of the day: Mona Lisa Wilson. Mona Lisa! Where did that name come from? I had spent my junior year of college in Europe. I had seen the Mona Lisa first-hand. And, this student sitting quietly in the back of the room appeared about as un-Mona Lisa-like as possible. The smile on the famous art subject has been described in many ways, none remotely resembling this Mona Lisa in my classroom. Much of the time, Mona Lisa Wilson hid behind the student in front of her, and when she was visible she covered her mouth with her hand. When a glimpse of her mouth was possible, it appeared sullen rather than any of the adjectives one would ascribe to da Vinci's model. Mona Lisa Wilson could only be described as a plain girl. She was about the same size as I and wore her hair closely plaited to her head.

For several weeks, Mona Lisa was a model student. She worked quietly on her assignments in her hidden spot. Her work was not outstanding, but she did work diligently. And she certainly never was a discipline problem, despite the rumors of her former teachers.

Mona Lisa's behavior was a relief because I was occupied with Liora. Within a few days, Liora began to flirt shamelessly with Todd. I would walk into the room to find her seated in his lap. Liora was cooperative when corrected, but her flirting was unstoppable. After a few weeks of school, I found that Todd was performing at a higher level than assigned. When I transferred him to another class, I thought the Liora problem was solved.

With Todd gone, however, Liora turned her attentions to Brent. Brent did not have Todd's maturity and confidence. He clearly did not know how to handle Liora's advances. The day I found her in his lap, confusion was registered clearly on his face.

I was astonished to see a middle school girl behave in this brazen way. Having student-taught in an inner-city high school, I had worked with students who had criminal records and students who had children. But middle school students seemed much younger and more innocent. And, besides, this was a rural school!

As I discovered, Liora was far from innocent. She was dating marines who were my age. I managed to keep her away from Brent, who was a true innocent. But I was perplexed about a child whose parents allowed her to date marines.

With these few hitches, the first grading period progressed fairly smoothly. Mona Lisa was passing. I began to emphasize oral skills. Students were required to give a certain number of speeches of specified types. Mona Lisa was reticent to participate in these activities, but she was not unique in this attitude. Few students had the experience or the inclination to speak in front of the class.

But "spelling baseball" was different. Everybody loved spelling baseball. As part of our spelling lesson routine, we held a spelling baseball game the day before the spelling test. The class was divided into teams, and each batter was given a spelling word. If the batter spelled the word correctly, she or he advanced a base. If the batter spelled the word incorrectly, she or he struck out. Words from previous spelling lessons could be used as well, and a batter could request a home run word from the challenge list. Spelling baseball was an active game. Students actually progressed around the room, and the nonbatting team placed players in the appropriate positions.

Mona Lisa was resistant to playing. She refused to "bat" when she was up. I forced her hand by threatening her team with a loss, but Mona Lisa was not happy about spelling baseball.

Then she began to miss school. Her excuses included washing day or watching the younger children. When certain crops came due, she missed school. Mona Lisa began to fall behind. She began to cause a disturbance in the back of the room. It was almost as though she were asking for my attention, as if she were saying, "I sat back here for nine weeks and you didn't ever pay any attention to me. Well, here I am and don't you forget that I'm here."

Her grades were plummeting; her work was deteriorating. I felt it was time for a parent conference. Mr. Richards agreed and we scheduled a conference. Mrs. Wilson, Mona Lisa, Mr. Richards, and I met in his office. I outlined my concerns emphasizing the academic. Mr. Richards turned to Mona Lisa and asked her to respond. Mona Lisa blurted, "She (meaning me) ain't no more grown than I am. She ain't the boss of me."

DISCUSSION QUESTIONS

1. What is this case about?
   a. What was the teacher's problem from her point of view?
   b. From your point of view?
2. What do we know about the teacher?
   a. What do we know about the teacher's personal background?
   b. What do we know about the teacher's training and previous teaching experience?
   c. Do you discern bias in the teacher on the basis of gender, race, or geographic location?
3. What do we know about the school and the community?
   a. How does the teacher describe the educational philosophy of the school?
   b. How does the teacher describe the community in which the school is set?
   c. What is the school's place in this community?
   d. How does the military setting impact the school and the community?
4. What do we know about Mona Lisa?
   a. How does the teacher describe Mona Lisa?
   b. What do we know about Mona Lisa's home life?
   c. Why do you think Mona Lisa behaved as she did?
   d. Do race, gender, or culture impact Mona Lisa's actions? Support your response.
5. What do we know about the other students?
   a. How does the teacher describe the twins?
   b. How does the teacher describe Liora?
   c. How does the teacher describe Todd?
   d. How does the teacher describe Brent?
   e. How do race, gender, or culture impact the teacher's views of the students? Did these views influence her actions?
6. What is your assessment of the teacher's decision to transfer Todd to another class? Should the teacher have taken further action regarding Liora? What would you do?
7. How could the teacher have avoided a showdown with Mona Lisa?
   a. Should the teacher have forced Mona Lisa to play spelling baseball?
   b. What do you think about the statement "I sat back here for nine weeks and you didn't ever pay any attention to me?"

   c. What do you think about the statement "Well, here I am and don't you forget that I'm here?"

   d. Should the teacher have called a conference with the parents?

8. What should happen next?

FOR FURTHER DISCUSSION

1. What was the culture shock the teacher experienced? Examining your own background, do you think you would have experienced the same shock she did? How can you prepare yourself for different cultural situations? Would you accept a position in a school where the culture was quite different from your own?

2. How important is it for the teacher's philosophy to match the school philosophy? The teacher to see "eye-to-eye" with the principal? Why?

3. Was Murraytown a true middle school? Support your answer with details from the case.

4. How does the Murraytown community compare to the rural community Mr. Boehm describes in "Starting in the Middle"?

5. How are rural and urban schools and students different from one another? How are they alike?

6. Was Murraytown a nongraded school? How do you reconcile the description of "nongraded environment" with the descriptions of the students that cite their grade levels?

FOR SCHOOL LEADERS

1. Which ISLLC standards apply to this case?

2. What should Mr. Richards's role be in the conference?

3. Should Mr. Richards have prepared the teacher for "culture shock"? How could he prepare her? How can a principal discern when a teacher needs preparation of this type?

CHAPTER THIRTEEN

Race Is Not the Issue

Titus Greene knew that race was a factor that had worked in his favor in obtaining his job as principal at Meltone Middle School. The school population was 95 percent African American and 90 percent free lunch. Test scores were at the bottom of the district and close to the bottom of the state. He knew if the scores didn't go up, he'd be walking in the spring.

His predecessor, Alton Stone, had been black, too. But Alton hadn't wanted to rock the boat. Alton had been passed over for some district-level positions, and he had measured his time to retirement at Meltone. He was a member of the community there, and it wasn't a big community. Everyone was related to everyone else and Alton wasn't going to muddy the waters. He just wanted to retire in peace. Alton had kept a tight rein on the students, but he let the teachers do whatever they wanted to do.

Titus couldn't afford to play the game that way. He was strict about teachers' lesson plans. He held their feet to the fire. If they wrote something in their plans, he expected to see that in practice. Titus was making good headway with most of the teachers, but Mrs. Settler was an enigma. She was the music teacher, and she just didn't conform to the rules. Music was a subject that most students would enjoy, but somehow Mrs. Settler managed to make it seem like drudgery. Mrs. Settler had been a problem from the beginning, but Titus had not expected what he heard in conference yesterday.

Several days ago, Lettie Gadsden had called him about her daughter's grade in music. Letitia was an honor roll student and had done well in all of her other classes, but had received a "C" in music. Titus called a conference. He would have done that in any case like this, but Mrs. Gadsden was an active parent in the school. She was president of the PTA and had participated in special student projects like judging for the Mayor's Writing Award. In the interim between the time Lettie had called and the day of the conference, Lettie's husband, Mack, had been elected to the school board.

Titus called Mrs. Settler in to inform her of the conference and to ask her how the grade had been determined. When asked for her grading scale, it appeared that Mrs. Settler had none. Mrs. Settler explained that grading in a subject like music was very subjective. Titus was not buying this response. He reached into his file drawer and retrieved a file with Mrs. Settler's long-range plans. There was nothing subjective in the grading scale outlined there, except perhaps for participation in class. Because of the nature of Mrs. Settler's instruction, the student work consisted mainly of quizzes and worksheets. The student work was not active or creative.

"How do you grade participation?" Titus asked.

"By whether or not they pay attention in class."

"How can you tell if they are paying attention?" Titus queried.

"By whether they look at me when I'm talking."

Titus balked. He was the kind of listener who had to dawdle or look at the ceiling to make the most of what he was hearing. He resented the presumption that she was making because he knew it didn't apply to him and it surely wouldn't apply to middle grade pupils.

"Do you have a record of Letitia's class participation grades?" Titus queried.

"Oh, yes. Of course I do."

"Could I see those grades?"

"Well, they're in my grade book."

Titus was surprised that Mrs. Settler had not brought her grade book to his office when he had informed her that he wanted to discuss a grade, but he was even more dismayed to find that her grade book was not even in school that day. Since he shared a music teacher with other schools in the district, it was several days later—the day of the conference—when Mrs. Settler returned with it.

Titus glanced at the daily participation grades. "These are the grades?" he inquired pointing to a long row of numbers. She responded affirmatively and he continued, "How does a student get a grade of 79 or 64 for participation?"

"Well, I've been using this system for years. It's in my head. It's always worked well for me."

DISCUSSION QUESTIONS

1. What is this case about?
   a. What was the principal's problem from his point of view?
   b. From your point of view?
2. What do we know about Titus?
   a. What do we know about Titus's personal background?
   b. What were Titus's views of education?
   c. What were Titus's motives for holding teachers' feet to the fire?
   d. Was Titus's primary role that of principal or politician?
3. What do we know about the school community?
   a. How would you describe the school community?
   b. How does the experience of the previous principal affect this case?
   c. Titus thought "Alton wasn't going to muddy the waters." Was Titus muddying the waters?
4. What are your views about Mrs. Settler's grading scale?
   a. Should participation be graded? If so, how?
   b. Is a class like music or art more subjective than math or language arts?
   c. Should the grading scale that is employed in a classroom match the grading scale specified in a teacher's long-range plans?
   d. How could Mrs. Settler's grading scale be improved?
5. What action should Titus take at the end of the case?
   a. How should the conference be handled? Who should attend? What topics should be discussed? Who should represent the teacher's position?
   b. How can Titus assist Mrs. Settler in clarifying her grading scale?
   c. How could he assist her in transforming her class from one of drudgery?
6. Is race an issue?
   a. What race is Titus?
   b. What race are the Gadsdens?
   c. What race is Mrs. Settler?
   d. If the Gadsdens are African American and Mrs. Settler is white, does race play a role?
7. Is Titus willing to sell Mrs. Settler out? Should he be allowed to change her grade? Was Titus biased against this teacher even before this incident?

FOR FURTHER REFLECTION

1. What is the principal–teacher relationship? Is it necessarily adversarial?
2. What role do test scores play in principal and teacher behavior? When Titus says that he knew "if the scores didn't go up, he'd be walking in the spring," what does he imply?

FOR SCHOOL LEADERS

1. Which ISLLC standards apply to this case?
2. Can you identify with Mrs. Settler's position? Can you put yourself in her shoes? Is it necessary to try to identify with the teachers when you interact with them?

CHAPTER FOURTEEN

I Started a Joke—On Myself

What had started as a joke wasn't real funny as I stood outside the assistant principal's office. I was wondering if I would still have a job when I walked out.

But it had started as a joke. On Tuesday, one of my chronically problematic eighth-graders had been a real pain. I had warned him once about his behavior, and when he misbehaved again, I gave him a demerit. In accordance with our school policy, I wrote out a demerit slip to deliver to his homeroom teacher. Tracking demerits is one responsibility of the homeroom teacher. If a student accumulates a certain number of demerits, she or he would serve detention or be referred to the office and so on.

I wrote Ramon's name in the designated space on the demerit slip, and in the "reason" section I wrote, "For being a shit." I knew that Marie, his homeroom teacher, would find this as funny as I did. She knew Ramon well. And Ramon wasn't supposed to see the demerit slip. Normal policy was that demerits were recorded and the slips themselves were destroyed. Demerit slips were never actually seen by the students.

Marie was distracted when I walked into her classroom. I could tell she was in a hurry. She looked at the demerit, chuckled and said, "Can you hold on to this until tomorrow? I'll get it then."

I held on to it, but apparently not tight enough because I, unknowingly, left it on a desk in my classroom. I woke up sick as a dog on Wednesday and was absent from school. Normally, an unexpected absence would have upset me because it would have interrupted my instructional plan. But I knew Wednesday's schedule included an assembly and the day would have been disrupted anyway.

While I slept blissfully through the day, Wednesday was being disrupted for me back at school. The demerit did *not* go unnoticed by the students in my class. And they passed it around during the assembly. Finally, one of my colleagues heard the chatter and retrieved the slip. As she took it from the student, the student said to her, "This says Mrs. Greenfield wrote this demerit. But I don't think Mrs. Greenfield really wrote that. I don't think she would do that. Do you?"

Ms. Shields looked at the note and replied, "Oh, my gosh, no. I don't think Mrs. Greenfield would write that. It doesn't even look like her handwriting."

Sally Shields saved me—sort of. She put the demerit in her desk drawer, checked with Marie, and then went to Dr. Lee, the assistant principal in charge of eighth-grade discipline. Like Marie, Sally found the note funny, but it wasn't funny to see it being passed around the assembly. Sally told Dr. Lee exactly what had happened. She implied that she had thrown the demerit away; however, she saved it for me.

Sally was on my team too. When, well rested, I waltzed in Thursday morning, I needed my strength. Sally caught me in the hallway and pulled me into the classroom. She handed me the demerit and said, "I took this from a student during assembly yesterday." She proceeded to explain what had transpired, concluding with, "And I told Dr. Lee about it."

My heart dropped to my feet. I turned red as the tomatoes in my garden. I thought, "What do I do. I'm being fired today. I can't afford to be fired today." I voiced, "What if I told her I didn't write it? If I said someone stole it and wrote it?"

Sally looked at me and said, " I think it's best to be honest."

I didn't like that answer one bit. "Has she seen the demerit?" I questioned. "No."

"I can lie to her then."

"I don't think that's a good idea."

As I walked to the office, a million thoughts flashed through my head. I needed my job desperately. Writing the note had allowed me to vent my feelings and go back to class refreshed. Did that justify my writing the note? Everyone else thought it was funny, too. It wouldn't be so funny if I lost my job. I poked my head inside Dr. Lee's door. When she beckoned me inside, I said, "Do I still have a job?" She looked me in the eye and said, "Did you write the note?"

DISCUSSION QUESTIONS

1. What is this case about?
   a. What was the teacher's problem from her point of view? From your point of view?
   b. What should the teacher do next?

2. What impact did the demerit have on Ramon?
   a. How do you think Ramon would have felt if he saw the note? Heard about the note?
   b. How do you think Ramon would feel if he thought the teacher really wrote the note? Another student wrote the note?
3. Should Mrs. Greenfield approach Ramon?
   a. What should she say if she talks to the student?
   b. What should the teacher say if Ramon asks if she wrote the demerit?
4. What kind of impact does the note have on the other students?
   a. Will the demerit influence students' attitudes toward Ramon?
   b. Will the demerit influence students' attitudes toward Mrs. Greenfield?
   c. What should Mrs. Greenfield say if another student asks if she wrote the demerit?
5. Was the note funny?

FOR FURTHER REFLECTION

1. Would elementary school students have reacted the same way about the note as the middle schoolers did? High school students?
2. In the "Catherine Conner" case, profanity was used by a student. In the current case, profanity was used by a teacher. Does permissibility differ by user? By profane words used?

FOR SCHOOL LEADERS

1. Which ISLLC standards apply to this case?
2. What action should the assistant principal take?
3. Would your viewpoint about the incident differ if you were a teacher?

CHAPTER FIFTEEN

I Can Handle the Children . . . It's the Parents I'm Not Sure About

I was amazed to be offered a job in one of the most prestigious schools in the area. I had just returned to my home state after completing a master's degree in education. The teacher training I received had been excellent. Between the training and a ten-year career in the pharmaceutical industry, I was confident of my subject matter and well prepared to interact with the seventh-grade students in my science classes. What I had not been adequately prepared for was parents.

Broad Street Middle School was set in an affluent community with a predominantly white upper-middle-class student body. Most of my disgruntled parent interactions stemmed from minor misunderstandings due to children being shuffled between divorced parents. But the biggest parent dilemma I faced was from an intact family.

After first quarter grades were disseminated, I received a telephone call from Mr. Langstrom who complained, "My daughter got a 'B' in science this quarter. Why didn't you call home if she was having trouble? She has *never* gotten a 'B' in class before. She always gets 'A's."

As I listened, I thought to myself: "No. I didn't call home. It's a 'B.' Why would I call home? I realize she's capable of 'A's, but she's a seventh-grader now. She's in that period of life. She got a 'B.' It's not so bad."

Mr. Langstrom continued, "I want you to change her grade."

As the words poured out of the telephone receiver, I wondered to myself, "Why would I do that? Why would I change her grade?"

Despite my thoughts, I responded politely, "I realize that Kimberly is capable of 'A' work, but I can tell you why she got a 'B.' She didn't turn in her assignments."

"Well, she was absent from school for a week with the flu," he responded.

"I know that Kimberly was absent, but she was still responsible for her assignments."

"She didn't know she had to make up the work."

As Mr. Langstrom spoke, I realized that I did not have a very good system for communicating make-up work to absent students. Thoughts about how to improve that system flashed into my mind. I replied, "I can understand how that might happen. I need to work on the make-up system. But Kimberly earned a 'B' and I am not going to change her grade."

We ended our conversation amicably. I assumed that Mr. Langstrom understood and accepted my explanation, but my assumption was in error. He complained to the principal who assigned the case to Mrs. Petty, a vice principal who was also my evaluator. Mrs. Petty called me to her office and asked me to explain the situation. As I neared the end of my recitation, I said to Mrs. Petty, "I can understand why maybe this girl didn't understand what she should make up because I didn't have the greatest system. But I've changed it now and this is what I'm doing." I emphasized that the new system would hold students accountable.

Mrs. Petty seemed satisfied and said that she was going to call the parent. "I'm going to put him on the speakerphone and let you listen. I don't want him to know that you're here though."

I was a little uncomfortable with the idea, but she was the administrator and my evaluator. I agreed.

Mrs. Petty dialed the number and reached Mr. Langstrom. She explained who she was and why she was calling. He launched into a tirade: "This is a crime. My daughter is an 'A' student. This 'B' is devastating to her. It has deflated her self-esteem. She just doesn't have any self-confidence. She's got a 'B' and her younger sister has all the 'A's. It's created a rift. Kimberly just doesn't believe she's smart anymore."

When Mr. Langstrom paused, Mrs. Petty said to him, "What do you want us to do about this?"

He answered, "I really want you to change her grade. She deserves an 'A.' I think the grade should be changed. It's the right thing to do. She didn't know about any make-up work. It wasn't made clear to her."

Mrs. Petty responded, "You might be right about her not knowing about the make-up work. Her teacher has developed a fine make-up system, but it's taken a while because it's the first year of teaching."

"That's obvious!" Mr. Langstrom interrupted before Mrs. Petty could complete her thought.

Mrs. Petty looked at me and silently mouthed some words. It was difficult for me to comprehend the gist of what she was saying and I couldn't really carry on a conversation without Mr. Langstrom knowing I was there. She muted the phone and said, "I'm going to go ahead and change your grade. It's just not worth the argument. Is that okay with you?"

What was I supposed to say? This was my administrator. And a parent. How big a stink could I make? How firm could I be with parents? My administrator? To what extent should students be held responsible?

DISCUSSION QUESTIONS

1. What is this case about?
   a. What was the teacher's problem from the teacher's point of view?
   b. From your point of view?
2. What do we know about the teacher?
   a. What do we know about the teacher's professional background? Teacher training? Previous teaching experience?
   b. How did the teacher view seventh-graders? Do you agree with those views? How does the teacher's view of seventh grade compare to that of "Catherine Conner"?
   c. What was the teacher's view of parent involvement?
3. What do we know about the school community?
4. What do we know about Kimberly?
5. What do we know about Mr. Langstrom?
6. What are some appropriate mechanisms for communicating make-up work to absent students? Why is a clear system important?
7. What do we know about Mrs. Petty?
   a. Of what import was it that she was the teacher's "evaluator"?
   b. Was it appropriate to use the speakerphone and not let Mr. Langstrom know? Why or why not?
   c. Should Mrs. Petty have mentioned that it was the teacher's first year of teaching?
   d. Was Mrs. Petty supportive of the teacher?
   e. Should the grade have been changed?
8. What do you think of the statement about Kimberly: "It has deflated her self-esteem"?
9. How do you think the teacher should have answered the question "Is that okay with you?"

FOR FURTHER REFLECTION

1. What do you think the teacher meant when the teacher said, "How big a stink could I make?"
2. How firm can a teacher be with parents?
3. How firm can a teacher be with an administrator? An evaluator?
4. To what extent should students be held responsible?
5. What is the teacher's gender? Do you think gender played a role in the interactions with the student, parent, administrator?
6. At what point should a teacher contact a student's parents when there is a change in grades?

FOR SCHOOL LEADERS

1. Which ISLLC standards apply to this case?
2. What was Mrs. Petty's role in this case?
3. How does an administrator balance support for a teacher with a valid parental complaint?

CHAPTER SIXTEEN

Principles and Principals

Earlier today, I had been in tears. Now I am just mad! And I still didn't know what to do.

Our school has a "kid-friendly" policy of never awarding the numerical grade of 69. Because 70 is passing, 69 is just too close to a passing grade. Lower grades can be assigned, but a 69 is taboo.

I agree with and appreciate the policy. It ensures clarity for students, parents, and teachers. If a 69 is not awarded, then nobody can complain about how close the grade is to passing.

The policy changes slightly at the end of the year. A final grade for the year can not be a 69 or a 68. The grade can be a 67 or a 70, but not 68 or 69. I understand. To fail a class at the end of the year with a 68 is hard to swallow. After all these are middle school students. Academics are important, but so is self-esteem.

Yesterday when I received my end-of-year grade verification sheets, I noticed that one child received a 68 for the year. His fourth nine-weeks grade was a 65, and when it was recorded his yearly average was automatically calculated at 68. I knew a 68 was not allowed so I played with the numbers. In order for him to receive an average of 70 for the year, I would have to *give* him a fourth nine-weeks grade of 85. 85! Instead of failing, as he actually had, that grade would imply he had a "B" average. On the other hand, in order to lower his grade to a 67, I had to drop the nine-weeks average six points. He was in an odd position and so was I. What I had to do in order to bump the grade to a 70 was not right, but neither was what I had to do in order to drop his grade to 67.

I queried as many other teachers as I could. I was not a first-year teacher, but I was new to this school. It was a suburban school where the student demographics had changed dramatically over the past several years. Once set in a fairly affluent neighborhood, a change in school busing routes had changed the average income level of the students' families to lower middle class. What did these other teachers think I should do? What did they think the principal would want me to do? The standard response was noncommittal.

My principles besiege me. One voice says, "Don't give him twenty points. It's not right. It's not right," while an equally loud voice chants, "You can't take points *away* from a student. It's not right. It's not right." Through my conversations with the other teachers, I had discovered that if the student didn't pass my class, he would not be going to high school next year. He had failed two other classes and only two could be made up in summer school.

I went to the principal this morning and said, "I am so sorry that I have to come to you with this but I have a situation here and I don't know what to do." I explained the situation to her.

She looked at me with her cold, concrete eyes and said, "You should have been able to determine beforehand that this was going to be a 68. You should have fixed it along the way. Now is not the time for you to come to me and give me this information."

"Fix it along the way." Those words rang in my ears. What did they mean? Did they mean that I should have been able to foresee the 68? Did she mean that I should have come earlier to speak to her? I knew it was late in the year. I knew things were down to the wire now—notifications regarding summer school and high school scheduling were being prepared.

"Could I have a little clarification," I requested. "Do you want me to drop the grade or give him twenty points?"

She looked me straight in the eyes with her frozen eyes—she must have won awards for "the stare" that teachers coveted and that cowed thousands of students. "Bernice, you cannot take points away from a student who has earned them."

"So you want me to add the twenty points?"

"Look, Bernice, I have finished talking to you about this. You need to go now."

When I hesitated to leave, she gestured me out of the room. I was mortified. I stumbled down the hallway toward my room. When I passed Mike Morgan's room, I decided he was the person with whom I should talk. Mike was an excellent teacher and well liked by everyone—including the principal.

I told Mike what had transpired. As I talked, I realized what had just happened to me. "She can't talk to me that way!" I exploded.

Mike agreed, "You're right. She can't talk to you that way. That's un-called for. *And* you don't need to walk from this situation feeling like that. Plus, you did your job. You asked all the teachers around you. You did what you needed to do before you went to her. Did you explain that to her?"

"Well, no, I didn't."

"You need to explain that to her. You need to go back and explain that to her."

I felt hesitant to go back, but Mike was firm in his belief. I knew Mike would not steer me in the wrong direction, so I mustered unknown courage and headed back to the office.

"I really don't mean to be a pain and I'm sorry to bring this back to your attention." I explained how I had consulted the other teachers and how the question still remained unresolved. I asked for her advice.

Her eyes turned to ice again and pierced my face. Simultaneously, her voice pierced the room. "Bernice," she thundered, "you don't need to be here again. We have already gone over this. I can't tell you what to do."

DISCUSSION QUESTIONS

1. What is this case about?
   a. What was the teacher's problem from her point of view? From your point of view?
   b. What should the teacher do next? What are the possible conse-quences of her action(s)?
   c. How do you think the teacher feels at the end of the case?
2. What are the teacher's opinions about the principal? Do you think her feelings affected her behavior? How?
3. What are your opinions about the grading policy?
   a. Is a grading policy like the one described in this case uniquely suited to middle school? Why or why not?
   b. What does it mean to say, "Academics are important, but so is self-esteem"?
   c. Which is the best course of action for the student?
4. What do you think about consulting other teachers to determine a course of action?
   a. What does Bernice imply when she says, "I was not a first-year teacher, but I was new to this school"?
   b. Was it useful for Bernice to ask the other teachers what to do?

5. What is the "stare"? Is it a useful attribute to cultivate? Why?
6. In "The Student with the Schedule," the teacher use "the stare." Does the appropriateness of usage differ?
7. Which is more important: principles or principals?
8. What lessons did Bernice learn for future grading practices? Future communication practices?

FOR FURTHER REFLECTION

1. Would you describe the teacher as a behaviorist, a developmentalist, a humanist?
2. To what extent do you think gender played a part in the interaction of the teacher and principal?

FOR SCHOOL LEADERS

1. Which ISLLC standards apply to this case?
2. What was the teacher's problem from the administrative point of view?
3. Were the principal's actions justified?
4. What were the principal's feelings about the teacher?
5. How would you handle the interaction with Bernice?
6. What actions could you take to "ward off" occurrences like the ones described in this case?

CHAPTER SEVENTEEN

The Evaluation

Evaluations are always a bit stressful, and I was readying myself for my second one as a student teacher. The first one, completed by my supervising teacher, had gone well. The second evaluator was a teacher that I admired, but at the last minute, I was informed that she wasn't going to be evaluating me after all. The assistant principal would be doing the one today. The news made me a little more nervous, but he wasn't coming until third period. I had second period to practice my lesson. I did; it went well; I began to calm down.

At the end of class, Ricky came to me and said, "Adam and Ron took my ring. They won't give it back."

I called Adam and Ron over and asked them to return the ring. It wasn't a valuable ring. In fact, I remembered it as something that looked like it came from a gumball machine. It had a stone in it and Ricky had shown it to me when we were studying rock formations. Ricky didn't appear upset; he just wanted it back.

Adam retorted, "I didn't take that ring from Ricky. Van gave it to me."

"Van, could you come over here for a second, please," I heard myself say. When I queried Van about what had been said, he stated, "Ricky told me I could give it to Adam to look at."

"Okay, where is the ring now?" I was getting a little annoyed.

Adam said that he had given it to Ron. Ron said that he had given it back to Ricky. Third period was nearing, and the assistant principal would be here soon. I suggested that the boys look for the ring. Adam and Ron became defensive, telling me that I could search their book bags if I wanted. They didn't have the ring.

"I am not going to look in your book bags," I stated as the assistant principal walked through the door along with the students from third period. "You find some way to work this out among yourselves. If that ring is not returned to Ricky by lunchtime, I will see you on the wall and in silent lunch (punitive measures)."

Adam said belligerently, "That's not fair. I told you I don't have it. Search me."

"Adam, it's time for third period. You need to leave now and go to your next class."

Adam started to speak up again, but this time the assistant principal intervened and told him to stop talking back and go to his next class.

In my mind, I had already decided what I would do if the boys had not settled the matter by lunchtime (eighth period). But in my heart-of-hearts I wanted the boys to work this out for themselves. If they didn't, I would suggest they apologize to Ricky, serve lunch detention, and write a 250-word essay about the topic "I will not take things that do not belong to me." It was a standard punishment.

I turned to third period and started the lesson. Again the students were responsive and I felt my evaluation went well. I honestly forgot about the ring incident until fifth period when I went to the team meeting. Their third-period teacher reported that Adam and Ron were upset when they came to class. I explained what had transpired. The teacher said that Ricky had not seemed upset at all. Adam was a quick-tempered youth who had had words with all of his teachers at one time or another. He was not unknown to the administration. Adam's temper usually dissipated quickly, though, and I assumed that he would be calm by lunchtime at eighth period.

The boys intercepted me as I left the room at the beginning of eighth period. I asked them if they had worked things out. Instead of being simplified, however, the story became more muddled. All of their stories changed and the final tale sounded like this: Ricky passed the ring to Dave (who had not originally been mentioned), who passed it to Van, who passed it across the aisle to Adam, who passed it to Ron, who threw it back to Ricky, who never received it. The boys vehemently argued their innocence. Meanwhile, my cooperating teacher, Mrs. Magwood, who had not been present earlier in the day, came into the room.

Ron said, "Hey, who is Mrs. Magwood calling. I saw her on the walkie-talkie."

"She's probably calling for Dave to come to the classroom," I replied.

The boys continued to bicker. I was on the verge of presenting my solution when Mrs. Magwood and the principal of the school walked into the classroom.

I don't know who was more surprised—the boys or me. I summarized the situation for the principal. Mrs. Magwood said that she was displeased with the boys for arguing with me. I remembered then that she had had several run-ins with Adam recently. I suspected she had just had her fill.

The principal asked each boy to describe what had happened. Each boy gave a different story, and each one gave a different version each time he was asked. I groaned inwardly. This should not have been such a big deal. Now it was escalating out of control. Eventually the principal tired of the bickering and told the boys to apologize to me for their actions and asked them to apologize to Ricky for losing his ring. He turned back to me and said, "Write these boys up with office referrals."

I really did not understand why these boys deserved an office referral. With the exception of Adam, they had been polite to me and to the other adults. I couldn't understand why Maggie Magwood had called the principal in the first place. She hadn't even bothered to get the details from me before calling. I couldn't question her with the boys and the principal there, and I sure couldn't refuse a direct order from him. I felt foolish for having gotten the principal involved and rotten that the boys would have office referrals. They probably felt that I had betrayed them.

As I wrote the boys up, they were quiet—except for Adam who began to argue with the principal. His was the only referral that cited disrespectful behavior. A few days later, the principal met with Adam's father because his behavior had generally deteriorated around the school. The principal reported to me that Adam's father had told him, in front of Adam, that he was taking legal action to disown his son. When I think about my second evaluation, I think about Adam. I am crushed that such a minor incident turned into such a huge hurt for Adam.

DISCUSSION QUESTIONS

1. What is this case about?
   a. What was the teacher's problem from her point of view?
   b. From your point of view?
2. What do we know about the teacher?
   a. How would you characterize this teacher?
   b. What was the teacher's gender?
3. How would you characterize the students?
   a. Describe Ricky, Ron, and Van.
   b. How does each typify adolescence?

    c. What reasons might you suggest for the behavior of each?

    d. What grade level were these students?

4. What do we know about Adam?

    a. How would you characterize Adam?

    b. How would you describe Adam's background?

    c. Is Adam a typical middle school student?

    d. How would you explain Adam's behavior?

    e. Did Adam deserve what he got?

    f. Do you think the ring incident contributed to the deterioration of Adam's behavior?

5. What role did the evaluation play in this case?

    a. What do you know about the evaluation system for student teachers in your own system?

    b. What is your opinion of the last minute change in the evaluator?

6. How would you characterize the other players in this case? What were their roles?

    a. Mrs. Magwood?

    b. The assistant principal?

    c. The principal?

    d. The team?

7. What is your opinion of the student teacher's solution to the ring dilemma?

    a. What is your view of the standard punishment?

    b. How did or could the student teacher's actions contribute to the boys working "this out for themselves"?

    c. What other interventions would you suggest for solving this dilemma?

    d. Could the student teacher have intervened earlier to solve the problem? How?

8. Do you think the student teacher should discuss this case further with the cooperating teacher? The principal? What should she say?

9. Would you describe the school as a "true" middle school? Why or why not?

10. What do you think about the student teacher's summation, "When I think about my second evaluation, I think about Adam. I am crushed that such a minor incident turned into such a huge hurt for Adam?"

FOR FURTHER REFLECTION

1. Do you anticipate any reaction by the parents of the boys who were referred to the office for the ring incident?
2. Was Ricky written up? Dave?
3. Did the student teacher overvalue the evaluation process and undervalue the students? Explain your thoughts.
4. What role does evaluation play in the student teaching/teaching process?

FOR SCHOOL LEADERS

1. Which ISLLC standards apply to this case?
2. Did the principal handle this case properly?
3. What follow-up action, if any, should the principal have taken with the cooperating teacher and the student teacher?

CHAPTER EIGHTEEN

Night and Day

PART A

Jordan felt just the same way as the sixth-graders did in Dr. Case's class example: "It was the happiest moment in my life. I couldn't believe it. I was so happy. I had waited so long for this moment and it was finally here." The student in the example was talking about the first day of middle school, and Jordan felt that way too. Today was *her* first day as a middle school teaching intern.

Jordan had finally made it to student teaching after several years of graduate school interrupted by the birth of her son and interspersed with a career change by her husband. She was placed in the exact school she had requested with the teacher she had requested. Jordan had met her cooperating teacher a few semesters earlier when she had observed Mrs. Speares teaching. Jordan was so impressed that she had come back repeatedly to observe Mrs. Speares. They were about the same age (Mrs. Speares was actually a year younger than Jordan) and had both matriculated through the same MAT program, so Jordan felt like they had a lot in common. And Jordan thought she could learn a lot from Mrs. Speares, who had been teaching only two and a half years but had wonderful classroom control and interesting and challenging lessons.

In their conversation last week, Mrs. Speares shared tales of her student teaching experience with Jordan. She had been abandoned by her supervising teacher and essentially had to "sink or swim." Mrs. Speares had had a horrible intern experience and she assured Jordan that she would do everything to ensure that Jordan's experience was not like her own. Mrs. Speares closed the conversation by explaining to Jordan that school started early. "Meet me in the school office. Be there at 7:10."

111

Jordan was a morning person and so excited about her first day that a 7:10 arrival was no problem. She waited, eagerly anticipating getting to know the students. At 7:20, students were admitted and sent to homeroom. Mrs. Speares rushed in breathlessly. Jordan greeted her with a cheerful "Good Morning." Mrs. Speares replied, "I am *not* a morning person!"

PART B

Jordan shrugged off Mrs. Speares's comment. It didn't seem important at the time. She was eager to get into the classroom. The room was filled with desks and book sets. Mrs. Speares's desk was in the back corner. Jordan glanced around. She didn't see a seat for herself. Mrs. Speares directed Jordan to the back of the class. In homeroom, Jordan listened to the discussion and starting memorizing names from listening to Mrs. Speares interact with the students. Mrs. Speares did not introduce her, but she thought it was an oversight. After class, Mrs. Speares hurriedly started making notes and gathering papers on her desk. Jordan did not want to interrupt.

In the next class, things were the same. There was no introduction of Jordan to the students. Jordan listened to class discussions and memorized student names. After class, Mrs. Speares resumed her flurry of activity. Jordan realized that she was planning the following class. Toward the end of the day, Mrs. Speares appeared more relaxed. She told Jordan to prepare an introduction for the students to be delivered on the next day.

When Jordan introduced herself to the students the next day, she made a special effort to speak to each one individually. She was pleased at how receptive they appeared toward the stranger in their midst.

For the remainder of that week and the entire next week, Jordan felt alternately neglected and in the way. Following a discussion with Dr. Case, she had managed to get her own space in the classroom. But Mrs. Speares was busy compiling her lesson plans during the day, or working on the talent show she was coordinating for the school. Jordan wanted to learn. She wanted to ask questions, but she was ignored. By the end of the week, Jordan was accustomed to Mrs. Speares's arrival pattern and began asking the vice principal to let her into the classroom before the bell rang. Her "Good Mornings" to Mrs. Speares were ignored. Jordan was aware that Mrs. Speares was not a morning person, so she didn't ask questions or speak to the students. She just wasn't sure how Mrs. Speares would react.

PART C

Jordan's preparation program had emphasized the middle school concept. She embraced it and especially the concept of teaming. In her methods class, groups of students were combined into miniteams and she could see the advantages of sharing information and strategies. Another thing emphasized by the teachers who had spoken to her class was the personal support provided by team members. Jordan decided that the team would provide a source of support and information. The team members were friendly—she called them all by their first names—and they were supportive on student matters. But she couldn't ask them about her biggest problem—her relationship with her supervising teacher.

Fifth period was Mrs. Speares's planning period. (She was still the only teacher Jordan did not refer to by first name.) By that time of day, Mrs. Speares thawed and Jordan was able to make inquiries about teaching techniques, classroom management, student performance and behavior, and various school policies. Some days Mrs. Speares would wax eloquent and talk effusively, but on other days she was brief and bustled out of the classroom.

Jordan felt isolated and uncomfortable in her role. She found herself looking toward the end of the day. She and Mrs. Speares had agreed on a date by which she would start teaching. That was her only ray of sunshine; she looked forward to the day when she could teach. Her rapport with the students was good; she felt comfortable with all of them.

But when it came, Jordan felt sabotaged by her teaching assignment. Mrs. Speares assigned her to teach grammar, something that Mrs. Speares, herself, did not like to teach. Mrs. Speares had covered grammar earlier in the year, but Jordan was not sure what she had taught or how. The first few days, Jordan found herself relying on Mrs. Speares to answer student questions because she wasn't sure of the previous grammar background.

Jordan had been reticent to share all of her concerns with Dr. Case. She had received the internship she had requested. She didn't want to alienate either her professor or her cooperating teacher. But she was desperate. Dr. Case listened intently. She met with Jordan and Mrs. Speares and suggested that they use a journal to communicate. Jordan could ask questions and discuss her concerns. Mrs. Speares could answer the questions and discuss her concerns. Either could express additional thoughts. Both agreed to try the system.

PART D

The journal functioned, but Jordan was disappointed that her relationship with Mrs. Speares was not close or comfortable. After a few days, Mrs. Speares no longer inhabited the classroom while Jordan taught.

Five weeks passed. During this time, Jordan made mistakes and learned from them. She continued to ask Mrs. Speares and the other team members for advice, but she began to feel like a real teacher.

One morning, Mrs. Speares appeared in homeroom. The class was in the middle of the Pledge of Allegiance when a minor disruption erupted. One student started laughing at another. Jordan had previously observed this same situation when Mrs. Speares was teaching, so she modeled her response after the cooperating teacher. She asked the two students to be quiet and pay attention.

After the pledge, Mrs. Speares addressed the class. "Why am I seeing this behavior from you recently? Do I have to be in the classroom all the time for you people to behave?"

Jordan felt her cheeks flush. What did she mean by "recently"? Jordan could not see any difference in the behavior of the students now from when Mrs. Speares had been teaching full time. She was furious.

Mrs. Speares returned later in the day. She asked Jordan to "be firm with the students so that I don't have to retrain them." She concluded her comments by saying that Jordan was too "bubbly" around the students, and they would not take her seriously if she appeared too nice. Jordan was crushed. She understood the rationale for the comments and she agreed to change her techniques, but she couldn't understand why behavior that was appropriate and worked for Mrs. Speares was not appropriate for her. She thought she had been acting properly by modeling Mrs. Speares, but Mrs. Speares did not see it that way.

DISCUSSION QUESTIONS FOR PART A

1. What is this case about?
2. What do we know about Jordan?
   a. How does Jordan feel about student teaching?
   b. How does she feel about Mrs. Speares as a teacher?

3. What do we know about Mrs. Speares?
   a. How would you describe Mrs. Speares?
   b. What do we know about Mrs. Speares's teaching internship?
4. How are Jordan and Mrs. Speares alike? How are they different?

DISCUSSION QUESTIONS FOR PART B

1. What is this case about?
   a. What was Jordan's problem from her point of view? From your point of view?
   b. What should Jordan do next?
2. Jordan stated that she felt "alternately neglected and in the way." Cite evidence for why she might feel the way she did.
3. How do you think Mrs. Speares felt about Jordan? Were her feelings and actions justified?
4. How does the title "Night and Day" describe Jordan and Mrs. Speares?

DISCUSSION QUESTIONS FOR PART C

1. What role did the team concept play in this case?
2. Why did Jordan feel sabotaged by her teaching assignment? Do you think her feelings were justified?
3. What do you think Mrs. Speares's thoughts were about Jordan as a teacher? Do you think they were justified?
4. Do you think Mrs. Speares was aware of Jordan's feelings of isolation and discomfort?
5. What is your opinion of the journal?

DISCUSSION QUESTIONS FOR PART D

1. How was Jordan's internship similar to Mrs. Speares's internship? How was it different?
2. Was it appropriate for Mrs. Speares to leave Jordan alone with the students?
3. Was it appropriate for Mrs. Speares to lecture the homeroom class?

4. What was Mrs. Speares's view of the behavior in the classroom? What was Jordan's view?
5. Was it appropriate for Mrs. Speares to talk to Jordan as she did?
6. What should Jordan do next?

FOR FURTHER REFLECTION

1. What roles did age, gender, and personality play in this case?
2. Should a relatively "inexperienced" teacher be allowed to supervise student teachers? When does a teacher become experienced enough?
3. Does modeling always work? Why or why not?
4. Can a teacher be too "bubbly"?
5. Do supervising teachers have to "retrain" their students? How can "retraining" be avoided?
6. Should an intern be allowed to request a student teaching placement? Should it be honored?
7. What constitutes good supervision?
8. Was the college supervision adequate? Why or why not?

FOR SCHOOL LEADERS

1. Which ISLLC standards apply to this case?
2. What is the role of school leaders in the training of future teachers?
3. Should the school administrator have been more knowledgeable or involved in this case?

CHAPTER NINETEEN

The Team

Mr. Beachat considered himself to be a forward-looking administrator. And he was ambitious, too. When he heard about the middle school concept, he embraced it as the right thing to do. He wanted to be the middle school principal of the year. He would make his junior high a middle school.

During the summer he reorganized his faculty into five-person teams. For each team, he assigned two language arts/reading teachers, a science teacher, a math teacher, and a social studies teacher. Mr. Beachat carefully selected team captains. He gave each team a name.

The Bears included the following five teachers:

- Betty, the team captain, was a history teacher. She had taught at the middle level for over fifteen years. She had a wealth of historical knowledge and students enjoyed the unusual, but true, tales that she told. She genuinely cared about her students but was a strict (and sometimes harsh) disciplinarian. Betty preferred the departmentalization of the junior high school to the new middle school concept.
- Laurie was one of the language arts/reading teachers. At twenty-five, she was in her second year of teaching. Although she had a well-defined weekly instructional routine and knew her content well, Laurie had difficulty with classroom control. Laurie liked the students so much that she just wanted to be friends with them. In addition, she was easily persuaded. Whereas that meant that she was receptive to new ideas, it also meant that she had been agreeable to leaving the school grounds without permission during her first year of teaching. Mr. Beachat wanted to ensure that Laurie was separated from the teacher who had encouraged her to behave unprofessionally.
- George was the other language arts teacher. George was the quintessential absentminded professor. He was a master of content, but often

had to be reminded to go to class. One time he sat through an entire parent conference without realizing it wasn't even a child he taught. George was a veteran of the old system. He wasn't entirely sure about this new middle school concept or his place on the team.

- Joe, another second-year teacher, taught science. Joe had just taken this position after an unhappy first year in a high school. Joe was open to the middle school concept and hoped that he could learn from his team. His high school experience had made him doubt his own abilities. He struggled with classroom control; he wasn't too consistent. Joe was easygoing and almost too willing to accept new assignments.
- Ms. Moss was the math teacher. Mr. Beachat knew that her name was Judy, but Judy did not allow anyone to call her by her first name. She was a veteran having taught some of the new faculty at the school when they were in junior high. Ms. Moss knew her content and was able to reach even "unteachable" students. She had coached academic teams in the past. Ms. Moss was eccentric though. Not only could no one address her by her first name, no one knew her birthday. She staunchly refused to be photographed. Ms. Moss liked to work alone. Departments were okay, but teams were a ridiculous idea.

While Mr. Beachat imposed the middle school model on his teachers, he continued to attend seminars. In one seminar he was introduced to six adopter types and how they managed change. Mr. Beachat studied his handout and classified his faculty.

Betty was not really a leader; she was late majority. George and Laurie were early majority. Joe was an innovator while Judy was a re-sister/saboteur.

Mr. Beauchat encouraged his faculty to try new, interdisciplinary ideas. George, Laurie, and Betty had formulated a depression unit. George had discovered that the play *Cheaper by the Dozen* was to be presented at a nearby community theater. At a team meeting, George suggested attending the play for a field trip.

ACTIVITY

Role-play the team meeting, acting out each person's response to George's suggestion. Make plans for the field trip and assign responsibilities.

ADOPTER TYPES

INNOVATOR	Eager to try new ideas, open to change, willing to take risks, naïve perhaps, not always an insider.
LEADER	Open to change but more thoughtful about getting involved, trusted by other people and sought for advice and opinions.
EARLY MAJORITY	Cautious and deliberate about deciding to adopt anything new; tends to be a follower not a leader.
LATE MAJORITY	Skeptical of adopting new ideas, set in their ways, can be won over by peer pressure and administrative expectations.
RESISTER	Suspicious and generally opposed to new ideas, low in influence and isolated from the mainstream.
SABOTEUR	Will not ever change position, will not cooperate and may try to undermine new ideas, person must be left behind as the rest of the group moves on.

DISCUSSION QUESTIONS

1. How would you classify yourself as an adopter type? Explain your reasoning.
2. Should teams be formulated based on adopter or other personality characteristics?
3. Can a concept like the middle school concept be imposed on a faculty? Will it work?

4. Should teams be assigned by the principal or should they be chosen by the members? What are the advantages and disadvantages of each approach?
5. Should captains be assigned or elected?
6. Should team names be assigned or selected by the members? Who should decide?
7. What are the implications for middle schoolers of a "harsh disciplinarian"?
8. Was Mr. Beachat right to separate Laurie from the other teacher?
9. What are the implications for middle schoolers of an "eccentric" teacher?

FOR FURTHER REFLECTION

1. How would you classify each of the teachers in this book?
2. Is classifying teachers useful to the everyday operation of a school?

FOR SCHOOL LEADERS

1. Which ISLLC standards apply to this case?
2. Do answers to the questions in the "Discussion Questions" section vary from the perspective of a school administrator or leader? Why?

Appendix: Standards for School Leaders

Standard 1: A school administrator is an educational leader who promotes the success of all students by *facilitating the development, articulation, implementation, and stewardship of a vision of learning that is shared and supported by the school community.*

Knowledge
The administrator has knowledge and understanding of:

- learning goals in a pluralistic society
- the principles of developing and implementing strategic plans
- systems theory
- information sources, data collection, and data analysis strategies
- effective communication
- effective consensus-building and negotiation skills

Dispositions
The administrator believes in, values, and is committed to:

- the educability of all
- a school vision of high standards of learning
- continuous school improvement
- the inclusion of all members of the school community
- ensuring that students have the knowledge, skills, and values needed to become successful adults
- a willingness to continuously examine one's own assumptions, beliefs, and practices
- doing the work required for high levels of personal and organization performance

Performances

The administrator facilitates processes and engages in activities ensuring that:

- the vision and mission of the school are effectively communicated to staff, parents, students, and community members
- the vision and mission are communicated through the use of symbols, ceremonies, stories, and similar activities
- the core beliefs of the school vision are modeled for all stakeholders
- the vision is developed with and among stakeholders
- the contributions of school community members to the realization of the vision are recognized and celebrated
- progress toward the vision and mission is communicated to all stakeholders
- the school community is involved in school improvement efforts
- the vision shapes the educational programs, plans, and actions
- an implementation plan is developed in which objectives and strategies to achieve the vision and goals are clearly articulated
- assessment data related to student learning are used to develop the school vision and goals
- relevant demographic data pertaining to students and their families are used in developing the school mission and goals
- barriers to achieving the vision are identified, clarified, and addressed
- needed resources are sought and obtained to support the implementation of the school mission and goals
- existing resources are used in support of the school vision and goals
- the vision, mission, and implementation plans are regularly monitored, evaluated, and revised

Standard 2: A school administrator is an educational leader who promotes the success of all students by *advocating, nurturing, and sustaining a school culture and instructional program conducive to student learning and staff professional growth*.

Knowledge

The administrator has knowledge and understanding of:

- student growth and development
- applied learning theories
- applied motivational theories

- curriculum design, implementation, evaluation, and refinement
- principles of effective instruction
- measurement, evaluation, and assessment strategies
- diversity and its meaning for educational programs
- adult learning and professional development models
- the change process for systems, organizations, and individuals
- the role of technology in promoting student learning and professional growth
- school cultures

Dispositions
The administrator believes in, values, and is committed to:

- student learning as the fundamental purpose of schooling
- the proposition that all students can learn
- the variety of ways in which students can learn
- lifelong learning for self and others
- professional development as an integral part of school improvement
- the benefits that diversity brings to the school community
- a safe and supportive learning environment
- preparing students to be contributing members of society

Performances
The administrator facilitates processes and engages in activities ensuring that:

- all individuals are treated with fairness, dignity, and respect
- professional development promotes a focus on student learning consistent with the school vision and goals
- students and staff feel valued and important
- the responsibilities and contributions of each individual are acknowledged
- barriers to student learning are identified, clarified, and addressed
- diversity is considered in developing learning experiences
- lifelong learning is encouraged and modeled
- there is a culture of high expectations for self, student, and staff performance
- technologies are used in teaching and learning
- student and staff accomplishments are recognized and celebrated
- multiple opportunities to learn are available to all students

- the school is organized and aligned for success
- curricular, cocurricular, and extracurricular programs are designed, implemented, evaluated, and refined
- curriculum decisions are based on research, expertise of teachers, and the recommendations of learned societies
- the school culture and climate are assessed on a regular basis
- a variety of sources of information is used to make decisions
- student learning is assessed using a variety of techniques
- multiple sources of information regarding performance are used by staff and students
- a variety of supervisory and evaluation models is employed
- pupil personnel programs are developed to meet the needs of students and their families

Standard 3: A school administrator is an educational leader who promotes the success of all students by *ensuring management of the organization, operations, and resources for a safe, efficient, and effective learning environment.*

Knowledge
The administrator has knowledge and understanding of:

- theories and models of organizations and the principles of organizational development
- operational procedures at the school and district level
- principles and issues relating to school safety and security
- human resources management and development
- principles and issues relating to fiscal operations of school management
- principles and issues relating to school facilities and use of space
- legal issues impacting school operations
- current technologies that support management functions

Dispositions
The administrator believes in, values, and is committed to:

- making management decisions to enhance learning and teaching
- taking risks to improve schools
- trusting people and their judgments
- accepting responsibility

- high-quality standards, expectations, and performances
- involving stakeholders in management processes
- a safe environment

Performances

The administrator facilitates processes and engages in activities ensuring that:

- knowledge of learning, teaching, and student development is used to inform management decisions
- operational procedures are designed and managed to maximize opportunities for successful learning
- emerging trends are recognized, studied, and applied as appropriate
- operational plans and procedures to achieve the vision and goals of the school are in place
- collective bargaining and other contractual agreements related to the school are effectively managed
- the school plant, equipment, and support systems operate safely, efficiently, and effectively
- time is managed to maximize attainment of organizational goals
- potential problems and opportunities are identified
- problems are confronted and resolved in a timely manner
- financial, human, and material resources are aligned to the goals of schools
- the school acts entrepreneurally to support continuous improvement
- organizational systems are regularly monitored and modified as needed
- stakeholders are involved in decisions affecting schools
- responsibility is shared to maximize ownership and accountability
- effective problem-framing and problem-solving skills are used
- effective conflict resolution skills are used
- effective group-process and consensus-building skills are used
- effective communication skills are used
- there is effective use of technology to manage school operations
- fiscal resources of the school are managed responsibly, efficiently, and effectively
- a safe, clean, and aesthetically pleasing school environment is created and maintained
- human resource functions support the attainment of school goals
- confidentiality and privacy of school records are maintained

**Standard 4: A school administrator is an educational leader who pro-
motes the success of all students by *collaborating with families and
community members, responding to diverse community interests and
needs, and mobilizing community resources.***

Knowledge
The administrator has knowledge and understanding of:

- emerging issues and trends that potentially impact the school community
- the conditions and dynamics of the diverse school community
- community resources
- community relations and marketing strategies and processes
- successful models of school, family, business, community, government, and higher education partnerships

Dispositions
The administrator believes in, values, and is committed to:

- schools operating as an integral part of the larger community
- collaboration and communication with families
- involvement of families and other stakeholders in school decision-
making processes
- the proposition that diversity enriches the school
- families as partners in the education of their children
- the proposition that families have the best interests of their children
in mind
- resources of the family and community needing to be brought to bear
on the education of students
- an informed public

Performances
The administrator facilitates processes and engages in activities ensuring that:

- high visibility, active involvement, and communication with the
larger community is a priority
- relationships with community leaders are identified and nurtured
- information about family and community concerns, expectations, and
needs is used regularly
- there is outreach to different business, religious, political, and service
agencies and organizations

- credence is given to individuals and groups whose values and opinions may conflict
- the school and community serve one another as resources
- available community resources are secured to help the school solve problems and achieve goals
- partnerships are established with area businesses, institutions of higher education, and community groups to strengthen programs and support school goals
- community youth family services are integrated with school programs
- community stakeholders are treated equitably
- diversity is recognized and valued
- effective media relations are developed and maintained
- a comprehensive program of community relations is established
- public resources and funds are used appropriately and wisely
- community collaboration is modeled for staff
- opportunities for staff to develop collaborative skills are provided

Standard 5: A school administrator is an educational leader who promotes the success of all students by *acting with integrity, fairness, and in an ethical manner.*

Knowledge
The administrator has knowledge and understanding of:

- the purpose of education and the role of leadership in modern society
- various ethical frameworks and perspectives on ethics
- the values of the diverse school community
- professional codes of ethics
- the philosophy and history of education

Dispositions
The administrator believes in, values, and is committed to:

- the ideal of the common good
- the principles in the Bill of Rights
- the right of every student to a free, quality education
- bringing ethical principles to the decision-making process
- subordinating one's own interest to the good of the school community
- accepting the consequences for upholding one's principles and actions

- using the influence of one's office constructively and productively in the service of all students and their families
- development of a caring school community

Performances
The administrator:

- examines personal and professional values
- demonstrates a personal and professional code of ethics
- demonstrates values, beliefs, and attitudes that inspire others to higher levels of performance
- serves as a role model
- accepts responsibility for school operations
- considers the impact of one's administrative practices on others
- uses the influence of the office to enhance the educational program rather than for personal gain
- treats people fairly, equitably, and with dignity and respect
- protects the rights and confidentiality of students and staff
- demonstrates appreciation for and sensitivity to the diversity in the school community
- recognizes and respects the legitimate authority of others
- examines and considers the prevailing values of the diverse school community
- expects that others in the school community will demonstrate integrity and exercise ethical behavior
- opens the school to public scrutiny
- fulfills legal and contractual obligations
- applies laws and procedures fairly, wisely, and considerately

Standard 6: A school administrator is an educational leader who promotes the success of all students by *understanding, responding to, and influencing the larger political, social, economic, legal, and cultural context.*

Knowledge
The administrator has knowledge and understanding of:

- principles of representative governance that undergird the system of American schools
- the role of public education in developing and renewing a democratic society and an economically productive nation

- the law as related to education and schooling
- the political, social, cultural, and economic systems and processes that impact schools
- models and strategies of change and conflict resolution as applied to the larger political, social, cultural, and economic contexts of schooling
- global issues and forces affecting teaching and learning
- the dynamics of policy development and advocacy under our democratic political system
- the importance of diversity and equity in a democratic society

Dispositions
The administrator believes in, values, and is committed to:

- education as a key to opportunity and social mobility
- recognizing a variety of ideas, values, and cultures
- importance of a continuing dialogue with other decision makers affecting education
- actively participating in the political and policy-making context in the service of education
- using legal systems to protect student rights and improve student opportunities

Performances
The administrator facilitates processes and engages in activities ensuring that:

- the environment in which schools operate is influenced on behalf of students and their families
- communication occurs among the school community concerning trends, issues, and potential changes in the environment in which schools operate
- there is ongoing dialogue with representatives of diverse community groups
- the school community works within the framework of policies, laws, and regulations enacted by local, state, and federal authorities
- public policy is shaped to provide quality education for students
- lines of communication are developed with decision makers outside the school community

Source: Interstate School Leaders Licensure Consortium (1996). *Standards for School Leaders.* Copies are available from: Council of Chief State School Officers. Attn: Publications. One Massachusetts Avenue, NW, Ste. 700, Washington, DC 20001-1431.

References

Aries, P. (1962). *Centuries of childhood: A social history of family life.* New York: Alfred A. Knopf.

Alexander, W. M., & McEwin, C. K. (1989). *Schools in the middle: Status and progress.* Columbus, Ohio: National Middle School Association.

Carnegie Council on Adolescent Development. (1989). *Turning points: Preparing American youth for the 21st century.* Washington, D.C.: Carnegie Council on Adolescent Development.

Colbert, J., Trimble, K., & Desberg, P. (Eds.). (1996). *The case for education: Contemporary approaches for using case methods.* Boston: Allyn and Bacon.

Demos, J., & Demos, V. (1969). Adolescence in historical perspective. *Journal of Marriage and the Family* (Nov.), 632–638.

Gillis, J. R. (1974). *Youth and history: Tradition and change in European age relations, 1770-present.* New York: Academic Press.

Hanawalt, B. A. (1992). Historical descriptions and prescriptions for adolescence. *Journal of Family History*, 17(4), 341–351.

Harrington, H. L., & Garrison, J. W. (1992). Cases as shared inquiry: A dialogical model of teacher preparation. *American Educational Research Journal*, 29(4), 715–735.

Interstate School Leaders Consortium. (1996). *Standards for school leaders.* http://ccsso.org.

Kett, J. F. (1977). *Rites of passage: Adolescence in America 1790 to the present.* New York: Basic Books.

National Commission on Excellence in Education. (1983). *A nation at risk.* Washington, D.C.: US Government Printing Office.

Neubauer, J. (1991). *The fin-de-siècle culture of adolescence.* New Haven: Yale University Press.

Shulman, J. H. (Ed.). (1992). *Case methods in teacher education.* New York: Teachers College Press.

Shulman, J. H. (1991). Revealing the mysteries of teacher-written cases: Opening the black box. *Journal of Teacher Education*, 42(4), 250–262.

Shulman, L. S. (1996). Just in case: Reflections on learning from experience. In Colbert, J., Trimble, K., & Desberg, P. (Eds.) *The case for education: Contemporary approaches for using case methods* (pp. 197–217). Boston: Allyn and Bacon.

Springhall, J. (1986). *Coming of age: Adolescence in Britain, 1860-1960.* Dublin, Ireland: Gill and Macmillan Ltd.

Index

ABOUT THE AUTHOR

Theresa G. Siskind, Ph.D., has been an educator at the middle school, high school, college, district, and state levels for over twenty-five years. She directed the Middle School Project at The Citadel, and is currently the assessment coordinator for the South Carolina Education Oversight Committee.

DATE DUE